WORLDING

Worlding:
Identity, Media, and Imagination in a Digital Age

David Trend

Paradigm Publishers
Boulder • London

Copyright © 2013 Paradigm Publishers

Published in the United States by Paradigm Publishers, 5589 Arapahoe Avenue, Boulder, CO 80303 USA.

Paradigm Publishers is the trade name of Birkenkamp & Company, LLC, Dean Birkenkamp, President and Publisher.

Library of Congress Cataloging-in-Publication Data

Trend, David.
    Worlding : identity, media, and imagination in a digital age / David Trend.
        p. cm.
    Includes bibliographical references and index.
    ISBN 978-1-61205-231-1 (pbk. : alk. paper)
    1. Internet—Social aspects.   2. Virtual reality—Social aspects.   3. Mass media and technology—Social aspects.   4. Identity (Psychology) and mass media.   5. Mass media and globalization.   I. Title.
    HM851.T776 2013
    302.23—dc23

                                                                    2012041198

Printed and bound in the United States of America on acid-free paper that meets the standards of the American National Standard for Permanence of Paper for Printed Library Materials.

17 16 15 14 13   1 2 3 4 5

CONTENTS

Preface
What Is Worlding?

Many of us think about a better world. But opinions may vary over how to get there, and especially about which "there" we want. The imagination and realization of worlds has become a driving force in "real" and "virtual" environments, with both negative and positive consequences. *Worlding: Identity, Media, and Imagination in a Digital Age* explores the many realms of experience we inhabit as we move back and forth between reality and representation in our daily lives. But in doing so, *Worlding* concentrates on ways of improving our common existence. As discussed throughout this book, "worlding" can be selfless or selfish. It can reinforce what exists or point to something else. But it can never be neutral. This book examines worlding as a word, an argument, and a possibility.

Worlding is a word. You won't find the term "worlding" in any dictionary, even though it has been in use for nearly a century. Martin Heidegger popularized the neologism in his 1927 *Being and Time* to mean "being-in-the-world."[1] The idea was to use a verb signifying something ongoing and generative, which could not be reduced to either a philosophical state or a scientific materiality. Since then, worlding has appeared dozens of times in philosophy, politics, cultural studies, and technology studies. The word has been appropriated and contested but never quite pinned down—and so retains a remarkable flexibility. In "Ways of Worlding," P. J. Rusnak catalogues many of the ways worlding has been treated in different disciplines and for varying purposes.[2] Noting the term's Heideggerian ontology, Rusnak cites worlding in discussions of colonialism and imperialism, secularism and faith, patriarchy and heteronormality, utopian and dystopian futurism, aesthetics and artistic expression, online networking and virtual community building, ecology and sustainability, proprioception and kinesthesia, and pedagogy and situated learning. Linguists have taught us that terms like "worlding" work less as fixed essences than as mediators of differences among the utterances and concepts around them. But this undetermined character hardly makes "worlding" innocent, deriving as it does from a noun referencing concepts of origins, boundaries, ethnicities, governance, and even consciousness itself. It is to this broad vision of worlding that this book is dedicated.

Worlding is an argument. World news, world record, World Bank—the list of "world" things is endless, generally conjuring up presumptions of totality or neutrality. But we know the limits of these conceits. Nothing using the term "world" is complete or neutral. The very slipperiness of the term means that it can be taken in negative or positive directions. To some, the word conjures images of sovereignty, while to others it might mean the creation a new domain. But in either case, "world" and "worlding" are loaded terms. For this reason, *Worlding* takes a stance within a field of indeterminacy—a stance against those who claim to have answers or certainty, especially those who prescribe to others. This is not the same as saying that values do not exist or that we even need to choose sides in an absolutist/relativist divide. *Worlding* takes the view that the divide itself is the problem, rooted as it is in an inherited binary consciousness that we struggle with every day in debates over good/evil, mind/body, center/margin, and so on. Without getting too philosophical about this, *Worlding* embraces the connection between thinking and being.

Worlding is a possibility. Disagreements over terms like "worlding" point to the importance of dialogue—the primacy of communication and the exchange of ideas. Put another way, worlding can be about ways we educate each other. The University of California–Santa Cruz's Worlding Project perhaps put it best in describing worlding as a "field imaginary" unbound by definition or convention, yet guided by curiosity and openness.[3] Worlding can be a way to critique an existing moment or a means to envision a utopian space that does not yet exist. This book is about the worlds we conceive for ourselves in relation to the world we find ourselves inhabiting. In other words, in this "world" thinking and being are not separated in ways that isolate or obfuscate complexity in the interest of expediency. Worlding is messy, indeterminate, and never ending. As such, worlding requires us to talk to each other and to always remember the limits of any perspective.

Notes

1. Martin Heidegger, *Being and Time,* trans. John Macquarrie and Edward Robinson, reprint ed. (New York: Harper Perennial Modern Classics, 2008).

2. P. J. Rusnak, "Ways of Worlding," Mind-o-licious, October 30, 2010, http://pjrusnak.wordpress.com/2010/10/30/designerly-ways-of-worlding (accessed October 30, 2012).

3. Christopher Leigh Connery and Rob Wilson, eds., *The Worlding Project: Doing Cultural Studies in the Era of Colonization* (Berkeley: North Atlantic Books, 2007).

Chapter One
Introduction

This book is about the worlds we visit in our minds and the ways these experiences shape our identities. The volume brings ideas about "virtual" places and societies together with perceptions about the "real" world in an era of mounting global uncertainty. Central to this project is the premise that virtual and real worlds are, in the final analysis, both products of mind and highly contingent on each other. This relationship between actual and imaginary worlds is the main concern of *Worlding*. Certainly the real world affects what we fashion in our imaginations, often providing a point of departure for fictional stories, adventure movies, and our most compelling computer games. But can virtual worlds have an effect on our actual day-to-day routines? Can stories and games help us fix real-world problems?

Virtual or Real?

At first glance, the connections between actual and virtual worlds might seem a bit vexing. One on hand, fictional worlds generally are set in seemingly realistic environments to make them appear plausible. Yet tangible experience can be depicted in ways that are anything but real. Factor in the differing ways we actually interpret what we see and hear, and the paradox of "worlding" becomes apparent. Variances in perception, culture, and literacy all enter the mix, demanding a recognition that the idea of a single "world" is at best an ideal and at worst a misguided delusion.

But this doesn't mean we can't make sense of it all. In fact, the many novel ways we possess of exploring fantasy landscapes and experiencing real-world events give us ever more potent tools for self-expression, personal insight, and, ultimately, intellectual growth. But it's a tricky business figuring out how to use these tools or even recognizing them when we see them. This book is about the transformative power of virtual experience and its role in shaping human identity. *Worlding* makes the case that new technologies we experience every day through our phones, computers, and other devices extend a primal desire to replicate the perceptions of the human mind in physical form—in an effort to step outside ourselves and witness the phenomenon of existence. This is especially the case in the new generation of immersive worlds presented by computer games. Through the illusion of leaving the everyday world and inhabiting a virtual environment, we have the ability to live out our ideals and engage in our "real" lives with fresh perspective and insight.

A growing number of thinkers now believe that computer games—such as those played by a whopping 50 percent of the American public—teach us new ways of thinking, which can benefit the world in concrete ways.[1] The important difference between these new virtual worlds and prior media experiences lies in the active role played by the viewer. In conventional stories and movies, one enters the virtual world in one's mind, but someone else scripts the actual experience. In the new virtual worlds, the viewer becomes the author of the story, actualizing the utopian vision and, in effect, living the dream. From this perspective the visitor to a virtual world has the radical capacity to look back on everyday experience and view it with fresh eyes—precisely because the utopian imagination always is a critique of the actual. Moreover, a growing number of computer games explicitly encourage players to directly engage and work to improve the nonvirtual world.

But none of this is easy. The instability of the worlds we carry around in our minds is heightened in an era of potent virtual experience. Movie special effects, sophisticated advertising gimmicks, immersive computer games, elaborate shopping malls, not to mention theme parks—all these offer a growing array of synthetic environments. Meanwhile, the world we consider the "real" one continues to be reshaped by human conflict, environmental change, shifting population demographics, urban renewal, and suburban sprawl.

In the "imaginary" world of stories and images, anything seems possible, as the illusionistic capacities of media and the Internet create ever more engaging narratives, games, and social networks. In the "real" world of people and places, things get bought and sold, actions have genuine consequences, and political events change the lives of people around the globe. Making things more complicated, these real and imaginary worlds constantly interact and influence each other. This means that keeping track of either world and remaining critically informed about each is a dynamic process in which the terrain is always shifting and the rules are continually changing. Conceptions of what is "imaginary" and "real" are fraught with debate, because the meaning of the terms can be unstable.

Worlding addresses the ways this evolution of our virtual and actual worlds has accelerated in recent years. The "imaginary" world has seemed to explode in its ability to render ideas into sounds and images, as well as in its creation of new platforms on which to fashion environments, human relationships, and novel forms of community. Meanwhile, events around the globe have reshaped the "real" world as never before, inverting traditional power relationships, redistributing populations and economic fortunes, and creating new paradigms of communication. As with any process of dramatic innovation and change, these events have had a mixed reception. Every celebration of the new world order and the emergent era of technological innovation has met a lament for fading tradition, values, and familiar ways of communicating.

Not that any of this is especially new. The interplay of real and imaginary worlds is as old as humanity itself—as are debates and suspicions about their relationship. The ability to represent ideas in symbolic forms like cave paintings is part of what distinguished early Homo sapiens from other creatures. From the earliest records of human reflection and philosophy, a mixture of wonder and discomfort has accompanied the impulse to make renderings of ideas and experiences. It is speculated that early humans attached magical beliefs to their depictions of hunting episodes on rocks and cavern walls—that somehow a picture of a desired quarry could bring it back again. Cultures around the globe would conceive religions and other belief systems that gave ideas form through ritual acts, images, and places of worship.

The human capacity to imagine has always been fraught with contradiction. As imagination has allowed people to imbue their thoughts with physical or oral form, products of the imagination have been contested throughout history as subjective or inauthentic. It seems we can never get a story or idea exactly right or render it in a way that satisfies everyone. Philosophers around the globe and throughout history have written about this curious disconnection between reality and perception. Plato and Parmenides pointed out that perceptions of the actual and the imaginary were different. Aristotle and Confucius observed that worldly experience was relative to the viewer. Siddhartha and Hegel added that our impressions change over time. Heidegger said that "the surrounding world is different for each of us."[2] And Freud complicated matters further by suggesting that we live not in a common world but in a common thought process. Things have only gotten more complicated as media and communications technologies have created ever more vivid ways of seeing the real world and imaginary alternatives to it.

Worlding and Identity

Worlding is a way of thinking about identity. Obviously we live in one big world of continents and oceans that exists in a planetary solar system of other worlds—which themselves inspire all sorts of real and fictional thought. But back on planet Earth, one might say that society creates certain kinds of worlds for us, each with its own set of rules and characteristics. Nations, states, cities, and towns form some of these worlds. So do families, groups of friends, schools, and workplaces. A category one might call institutional worlds includes the stock market, the National Basketball Association, and the Catholic Church. Then there are worlds that exist only on paper or in electronic form, which configure themselves in our minds: children's stories, news reports, TV shows, movies, e-mails, Facebook, Twitter, *World of Warcraft*, and so on.

All these many worlds are defined by boundaries and rules. Here is where worlding gets interesting. Because worlds generally correspond to groups of some kind—like populations or casts of characters—they are characterized by inclusions, exclusions, and the reasons or criteria through which group membership is defined. Narratives often hinge on a tension between insiders and outsiders, competing groups, or individuals in some kind of relationship to a group. Think of all the stories that emerge from issues of belonging, cooperation, competition, or conflict between groups defined by social class, nationality, race, gender, or where members live. Boundaries of worlds can cause tensions, as seen today around the globe in disputes over territory, governance, resources, rights, and immigration. Equally important are the rules that govern worlds. Just as laws and regulations structure everyday social behavior, story and game worlds are similarly organized. A player can't begin to function in *Halo, Resident Evil,* or *Spore* without a knowledge of how to proceed.

The boundaries and rules of worlds—both real and virtual—are defined by belief systems: the consensus of understandings and values of those using or populating each realm. Obviously everyone inhabiting a municipality tacitly agrees that traffic laws need to be enforced. And a democratic political system implies that citizens have mutually decided what those laws dictate. But things aren't that simple. As suggested above, the ways that worlds operate are subject to change as the beliefs and values of constituents shift over time. In the world of a computer game, rules can be updated or violated, or the world can be abandoned. In the civic arena, laws and government regulations undergo continual contestation and revision. Even the ways people treat each other in the worlds of families, work, and school continually shift and change.

Worlding is about this process of change—about the things that influence the boundaries and rules that affect individuals, groups, and the dynamics that define their worlds. It might be easier to say that this is a book about "ideologies," or the belief systems that hold worlds together. But that wouldn't be quite accurate. The concept of ideology always has had difficulty dealing with the communications envelope that surrounds it. An entire theoretical literature has tried to explain how sign systems, language, and media influence or fail to influence the way people see their worlds and treat each other. But most of that literature has failed to explain those processes adequately. More to the point, worlding today is significantly more complex than it was in the distant past or even as recently as a decade ago, now marked by new economic and political realities, enhanced media and technological capabilities, and people's growing abilities to experience worlds like those offered by cell phones, satellites, the Internet, and digital visualization.

Worlding and its premises emerge from current discussions in philosophy, art, media studies, literary theory, sociology, education, and political science. Such intellectual discourses generally evolve their "new" findings from incremental refinements of insights developed over long periods. If there is a novelty to the concept of worlding, it lies in its synthesis of existing concepts. Each chapter of this book will detail prior thinking on the topics it discusses and then relate these ideas to interdisciplinary principles of real and virtual experience. This book addresses these growing complexities as manifested in seven areas.

Chapter 2, "World Systems of Thought," addresses the philosophical dimensions of worlding, examining various concepts of the "real" world and the ways mental impressions of the world have varied and evolved over time. Topics include perceptions of the self in the world, states of consciousness, cross-cultural belief systems and religions, and the roles of science and creative expression. Utopias figure prominently in many world cosmologies by reflecting individual and collective attitudes toward the past, present, and future.

Chapter 3, "Consuming Desires," discusses the inevitable role of consumption and trade in worlds of all kinds. Real-world economics manifest themselves most commonly these days in the interface of market capitalization and democratic politics, often with contradictory implications. In a society that encourages competition and individualism, ideals of community and the common good become devalued. The acquisition of things for private enjoyment supplants appreciation of human values like compassion and sharing and, ultimately, of society itself.

Chapter 4, "Mapping Media," begins with the simple premise that world geographies are mapped and divided. But in the context of this book, such worlding has become virtual or ephemeral, largely due to technology, but not completely so. Entertainment media and other forms of digital communication allow people to know and experience more than ever before, but always through some mediating interface, some kind of gateway or filter, that has the capacity to limit or manipulate the experience.

Chapter 5, "Destination America," uses a recently built "theme mall" in California as a point of departure for a broad-ranging discussion of cultural politics, urban planning, and the American Dream. In this instance a small bedroom community found itself powerless to resist the expansive imperatives of a notorious commercial developer bent on replicating a Disney-like world in the midst of several multiethnic, working-class neighborhoods.

Chapter 6, "Virtual Culture," looks at the human drive for immersion in imaginary worlds—from ancient yarns and childhood stories to contemporary movies and computer games. Our desire for ever more convincing "virtual" experience can be seen throughout the history of art and representation. What drives this desire? More importantly, can immersion in artificial realities have an effect on what we perceive as the nonvirtual world? This section of *Worlding* argues that neat separations of "real" and "imaginary" need to be discarded in favor of an integrated understanding of the way these realms blend and interact with each other.

Chapter 7, "The Mean World," describes the workings of authority in actual and virtual worlds. Power can become a misunderstood concept—in that its ubiquity in everyday life ironically can make it invisible. Everyone's life is shaped by local and national government, as well as the power exerted by an employer or educational system or the sorts of control related to one's income, age, gender, or ethnicity. Yet individuals also have power, although it is often unrecognized or undervalued. How do we connect the power of individuals to larger structures?

"Globalization" is that often abstract term for our larger world and its systems. Often people have difficulty imagining their relationship to an entire planet. Yet the connection is inescapable. Chapter 8 discusses both the nature and variety of those connections, as well as the ways technology continues to reshape our relationship to the larger world around us. Do global capitalism and trade improve or harm the world? Does the Internet bring us closer together or foster isolation? Can improved means of communication make the world a better place? These are all open questions. But, as I will suggest, we are hardly as powerless or disconnected from each other as some suggest. All we need is the will to fix our world.

From what I just outlined, it might be reasonable to conclude that *Worlding* is a product of pessimism. But that isn't the case. None of the matters I have raised are settled or closed. Nothing is etched in stone. In fact, there is plenty of evidence to suggest that growing numbers of people are so frustrated with the current state of affairs that they are clamoring for change. Witness the enormous resentment expressed in recent years toward fat-cat corporate CEOs collecting big bonuses and the anger about congressional gridlock and political incumbents in general. In response, new grassroots movements and forms of political alliance are popping up all around the globe. In America's recent recession, we witnessed rises in anti-immigrant sentiment and reactionary outbursts. Yet we have also seen a remarkable outpouring of tolerance and generosity in new social movements, especially among the ranks of young people.

Empirical evidence bears out much of this good news. Despite recent economic trends, world hunger and suffering have fallen to their lowest levels of the century.[3] For decades, both crime and international conflict have been declining.[4] Meanwhile, all over the world groups are organizing for humane purposes and for positive social change in an unprecedented way.[5] Explanations vary as to why so much good is occurring. Some point to the economic depressions of the past and the way hard times have inspired generosity and kindness among so many. Others suggest that communications technologies like the Internet are fostering new forms of connectedness.

Whatever the explanation, we can do better than knee-jerk "take-back-my-country" sloganeering or thinly veiled xenophobia. Democracy in the United States and around the world can succeed if the right balance is found between individual and collective interests—and if an understanding of this balancing act is widely appreciated. Such understanding isn't automatic, and it isn't exactly an easy process in today's society. This book is about this search for a better future.

Notes

1. Jane McGonigal, *Reality Is Broken: Why Games Make Us Better and How They Can Change the World* (New York: Penguin, 2011).

2. Martin Heidegger, *Basic Problems of Phenomenology* (Bloomington: Indiana University Press, 1982).

3. Peter Singer, *The Life You Can Save: Acting Now to End World Poverty* (New York: Random House, 2009); Charles Kenny, *Getting Better: Why Global Development Is Succeeding—and How We Can Improve the World Even More* (New York: Basic Books, 2011).

4. Fareed Zakaria, *The Post-American World* (New York: W. W. Norton, 2008); Mark Milloch-Brown, *The Unfinished Global Revolution: The Pursuit of a New International Politics* (New York: Penguin, 2011).

5. Paul Hawken, *Blessed Unrest: How the Largest Movement in the World Came into Being and Why No One Saw It Coming* (New York: Viking, 2007).

Chapter Two
World Systems of Thought

Let's face it: the "real" world is a pretty big place. The sheer size of the planet, the scale of global problems like hunger and war, the enormity of bureaucracies and governments—all these things can make us feel small and powerless. No wonder more than a few current thinkers have written that "reality is broken."[1] No wonder more and more of us find solace and connection through "virtual" worlds or alternate realities. It's important to remember that this tendency is hardly a new occurrence. Throughout history and our own lives, we human beings have found something important in stories. We are sustained by the ways our minds take us to "imaginary" worlds.

The question is this: At times when reality seems broken, are our journeys into virtual worlds good or bad? Can we benefit from these travels into the imagination, or are we merely escaping from things we should be addressing? Part of the purpose of this book is to take an unflinching look at the very "reality" of the problems facing the planet, to acknowledge the fact that many things are not going well. But the other purpose of this book is to argue that the human capacity for "imagination" has always helped us through difficult times—as a way not to escape problems but to develop solutions to them. Throughout history, inventors, philosophers, political thinkers, and many of our greatest scientists have all reached the same conclusion: our capacity for imagination is our greatest gift. Imagination is what sets us apart from other species. It can help us visualize yet-unrealized solutions. It can help us see a better future. Imagination can save the world.

The challenge of imagining a better world begins with everyday life. This means looking beyond the abstract theories of intellectuals lost in time to the concrete ideas undergirding much of what we think and do. As I explain this in a bit more depth, it's important to point out that what I'm writing about isn't exactly new or original. Questions of worldview, perspective, bias, and ideology are, after all, the cornerstones of philosophy and humanistic inquiry. These matters also lie at the heart of every academic discipline and field of inquiry. For example, scientific literature has for decades wrestled with questions about objectivity in research protocols. Careful attention is paid to separating biases and preconceptions of scientists from the "objective" findings they seek. Social science similarly has scrutinized the role of a scholar's own identity in coloring research outcomes. Do men and women look for different details or ask different kinds of questions? What effect does the presence of anthropologists have on primitive people they encounter? Do research subjects act differently when they know they are being watched?

Can we say that there are general principles about the ways people think that apply across these intellectual fields? Philosophers have cautioned against the idea of "universal" rules of human behavior because there is so much variance in societies around the world. Certainly this is something to keep in mind. Consequently, while this book takes an interdisciplinary approach to addressing broad questions of human thinking about real and imaginary realms, attention is paid to vital differences in the ways people experience their "worlds."

Time and Memory

Time matters. Some people argue that time is the most valuable commodity in life. After all, each of us has only so much of it. As children we soon learn to live by the clock, understanding that our lives are organized by schedules, with times assigned to school, home, and play. Later we sell our time to employers and save up leisure time. People with resources can buy things like appliances and cars that help them save time. Think about the time expended by commuters waiting for buses or the hours spent in traffic by people who can't afford homes near their jobs. Entire labor categories like babysitters, domestic workers, and home-cleaning services exist so that people with resources can have time to pursue their careers or other interests.

The ways we think about events in time are subject to influence and change. History as an academic discipline is part of the basic school curriculum. It forms the common body of information that societies share so that they can apply the lessons of their past as they move through the present. Yet many educators and policy makers now worry that growing numbers of people are failing to acquire historical knowledge. Debates on education have often become very heated over the quality of student historical knowledge. Two decades ago, E. D. Hirsch famously observed the "cultural illiteracy" of American teenagers unable to recite key historical names and dates.[2] Hirsch opined that the very fabric of American society was in peril because the nation's collective past was being forgotten.

But in today's world such worries over names and dates really miss the point. Information overload in people's lives drives human consciousness increasingly into the here and now. The speed and immediacy of communication have become both an enormous force for social good and a nagging problem. We can know instantaneously about events in the lives of our friends and those we don't know. We can get answers and head off misunderstandings. But the massing of real-time data in our minds squeezes out memories of what happened a few months, years, or decades ago.

Consider the many ways we receive information every day: text messages, e-mails, phone calls, video, TV, movies. Then add the daily barrage of billboards, print advertisements, newspapers, magazines, and books. Finally, consider the endless volumes of knowledge exchanged in conversations with friends and family, instruction from teachers, communication with employers and coworkers. It's an enormous amount to take in—and often it's hitting us all at the same time. Of course, this problem is neither new nor newly recognized. The growing immediacy of human consciousness is built into the evolution of media itself—from the printing press to the iPhone. Moreover, we can't simply attribute this shift in human consciousness to technologies. Media innovations are components of larger cultural systems, which link to the understandings and purposes humans attribute to such technologies, their social functions in supporting individuals and groups, the economic and business models that animate the technologies, and the various kinds of content delivered. Together these components fuse to comprise what Henry Jenkins has termed "convergence culture."[3]

As convergence culture continues to intensify, it produces an ever more complicated information and entertainment system—in other words, there is more and more to follow, intellectually and experientially. As a result, things can drift into the past and get forgotten more easily. While E. D. Hirsch may lament that some tenth graders can't quite place Alexander Hamilton, just try asking him to identify Adele or Ludacris. The more serious problem comes when tenth graders can't identify current congressional leaders or the vice president.

Worlding is one way of making sense of convergence culture. But to use worlding for this purpose we need a full toolbox of conceptual strategies. Worlds are products of the mind, whether we are discussing imaginary or real domains. Our perceptions of worlds have been the subject of human discourse, art, and philosophy since the beginning of civilization. This chapter maps out some of the ways influential thinkers have modeled those worlding methods, then links these intellectual traditions to the situation we find ourselves in today. We inhabit a moment of remarkable possibility, when human consciousness about the real world as a community has been enhanced by network and satellite technologies. At the same time, our capacities to imagine and even rehearse a better world may never have been more accessible or vibrant. With this in mind, we move from a review of worlding philosophies to a discussion of the ways humankind has imagined its world in relation to the larger celestial universe.

Finally, any treatment of worlding must address the concept of utopia—and all the positive and negative associations that go with it. From the beginning of recorded thought, people have used their capacities in language and mark making to imagine worlds different from the here and now. When Thomas More coined the term "utopia" in the 1500s, he gave a name to a kind of thinking about a better world. While utopian thinking has often become associated with unrealistic dreaming, many now argue that it retains relevance in keeping alive human ambitions that can motivate people toward genuine social change.

In common usage, "world" signifies the planet we occupy or the totality of human life upon it. In the English language, the word "world" evolved from *weorold,* meaning "age of man," which can be traced to the Old Saxon expression *werold* with a similar meaning.[4] The Latin word for world, *mundus,* can be traced to the Greek *cosmos,* both of which refer to the act of establishing "order out of chaos." In most of its linguistic manifestations, "world," or, as I am using the term, "worlding," references the human impulse to conceptualize or make sense of a surrounding totality, either on Earth or in the greater universe. Of course, "world" also has numerous philosophical meanings, since our conceptions of what surrounds us are always a function of our minds. Perception, upbringing, belief systems, and media all play a role in our ideas about the world. And, of course, some scholars have argued that certain nations and peoples have dominated others through conceptual models of "worlding," which validate their positions of power and authority.[5] Finally, in contemporary times we have come to ponder the possibility of other worlds, whether those worlds exist on other planets or in the imaginary landscapes rendered in books, movies, or virtual environments.

Knowledge Domains

This book seeks to make sense of this broad terrain of worlding by examining the many ways we experience our surroundings. While this may sound like a daunting task, it isn't quite as unmanageable as one might initially assume. Worlds, whether in physical space or the imagination, follow certain rules of definition, design, and operation. And as products of human consciousness, worlds also emerge from identifiable thought processes and beliefs. So we begin by discussing how different disciplines or schools of thought, such as science, the humanities, and the arts, see worlding. From there it is important to discuss worlding as a philosophical topic or product of the mind—sometimes termed "cosmology"—and the ways people have articulated mental images in language, stories, and pictures. Finally, we explore how all of this relates to our everyday lives, the places we live, and the ways we imagine the future ahead of us.

Natural Science

To explore ideas about real and imaginary worlds, one must consider natural science and the character of the planet we call Earth. The so-called third rock from the sun (of eight planets) is home to millions of biological species and the only planet known in verifiable terms to host life. And despite the realities of environmental pollution and potential nuclear destruction, our Earth is projected to be suitable for supporting life for at least another 500 million years.[6] Later in this book, the topics of physics, planetary bodies, and celestial worlds are discussed in depth because they figure so prominently in religion, storytelling, and the popular imagination. Suffice it to say that the work of seventeenth-century physicist, mathematician, and theologian Isaac Newton set forth a series of principles about gravity, motion, and the solar system that altered human understanding of the "world." Newton's thinking holds special significance for this book in that he introduced a set of "rules" defining underlying systems that govern the way our world works. All real and imaginary worlds rest on such governing principles, whether they are discovered by scientists or devised by writers. Thinkers throughout history have focused on the relationship between science and nature, often seeing an oppositional relationship between the two. In the nineteenth century, biologist and naturalist Charles Darwin refuted this dichotomy with his explanation of the evolution of living species, which sought to provide unified theories applicable to all creatures on Earth. Darwin's "worlding" principles would eventually be challenged, as when his theories of evolution were deemed overly general to be applied to human beings.

Science is often seen as the opposite of philosophy and faith. After all, scientific reasoning emerged in the Enlightenment era as civilization was searching for rational explanations for phenomena once thought to be caused by magic or gods. Faith is abstract and ephemeral; science is concrete and verifiable. Or so it seems. Scientific principles are often revised over time, even ones thought to represent unchanging facts. In the twentieth century, questions began to arise with increasing frequency regarding common assumptions that science is a neutral pursuit, with many thinkers concluding that science often reflects self-serving human interests. Famously, this opposition between human interest and the natural world is popularized in the blockbuster *Avatar* movie series (2009–2016), in which profit-hungry human explorers exploit the natural resources of another planet.

We look to science to solve many of the world's problems by curing diseases, improving our diet, increasing our efficiency, and helping us to communicate better. Science also helps us predict what lies ahead. And in recent decades scientists have been telling us that our world is in trouble. The *Avatar* series and similar movies dramatize a growing scientific concern over the future of the Earth and the limits of its resources. Between 1950 and today, the world's population more than doubled, from 2.5 billion to 6.8 billion people. World population is expected to increase by approximately 90 million per year through 2050.[7] In recent decades concern has grown over the physical limits of global resources, particularly in terms of water and oil. Although oceans cover two-thirds of the Earth's surface, methods for removing salt from seawater remain expensive and thus impractical for satisfying the planet's freshwater needs. Agriculture accounts for 70 percent of world water use, with industrial and household consumption each taking 15 percent. In geographical terms, water is most available in North America, Europe, and northern Asia—leaving South and Central America, Africa, southern Asia, and Australia with water challenges. About half the world's population lives with a piped source of water to homes, with 40 percent existing without modern sanitation systems and 20 percent with no natural water supply at all. Water pollution can make matters worse. For decades homes and industries released sewage and manufacturing waste into water sources without restraint, fouling many rivers and lakes. Contaminants from agricultural insecticides, herbicides, and fertilizers created further problems. Until environmental regulations put a stop to such practices, the waters of the American Great Lakes were infamous for being undrinkable and hazardous to swimmers. In addition to such pollution by human beings, other natural factors ruin water. Some of Africa's most desperate countries have water supplies ridden with bacteria and insects. Shortages of water most directly affect food supplies. According to the United Nations, twenty-five thousand people die of starvation every day.[8] Approximately 800 million are undernourished, a number that has grown with the outbreak of blight that has decimated wheat fields in Africa and Asia.

The world's energy crisis is also no secret. Lack of water may be the most direct threat to life on Earth, but oil gets more public attention. While in recent years much has been done to help lessen the consumption of oil and gas in transportation, home, and industrial use, tremendous amounts of petroleum are still used in agriculture, mostly in the production of fertilizers. Decreases in oil supplies can cause higher food prices and produce famines in poor or highly populated countries. By some current estimates, to return to a sustainable level of consumption and avert an oil-related threat to humanity, the US population would have to be reduced by at least one-third and the world's population by two-thirds.[9] Oil spills have produced another kind of petroleum-related environmental problem. Until the mid-1990s, tanker ships ruptured on a regular basis, often releasing millions of gallons of oil into oceans. Some spills took months or even years to clean up—a reality that reached an unprecedented scale with the rupture of British Petroleum's *Deepwater Horizon* well in the Gulf of Mexico. As the world looks to the future of oil consumption, one central issue remains unresolved: no one knows for certain how much oil remains to be extracted from the Earth. Various interests in the oil debate offer quite contradictory estimates of how much oil exists and how long the world can continue consuming it. The Organization of Petroleum Exporting Countries asserts that the total amount of oil in the world is 1.3 trillion barrels, an amount we will exhaust in thirty to forty years at current consumption rates if no new oil deposits are discovered.

Social Science

The study of human beings began in earnest during the Enlightenment. In the 1500s royal authority, tribal politics, and class status began to give way to a society organized around personal achievement, money, and eventually demo-cratic principles. Amid these changes, "rational" inquiry began attempting to take the mystery out of the human condition by explaining how people think and behave—in the so-called social sciences. Popular revolutions in Europe, the Americas, and elsewhere in the 1700s abolished power formerly held by kings and queens, as printed texts enabled populations to share information about their collective interests and organize politically. The discipline of history emerged as accounts of past events could be published and shared, giving populations a crucial understanding of their identities and legacies, while allowing them to appreciate the role of prior achievements, alliances, and conflicts in the develop-ment of their current conditions. From this drive to understand human history came archaeology, which examines past civilizations, and anthropology, which looks at human societies and their relationships to their shared environment.

In the context of this book, social science redefined "worlding" as something that could be boiled down into discrete categories like economics, education, linguistics, political science, psychology, and sociology. While philosophy and theology had for centuries offered abstract explanations of the order of the world and the universe, social science promised concrete analysis predicated on practical evidence and everyday reality. In this sense, each social science discipline fashions its own kind of "world." Economics does this by arguing that human society is organized by the creation and exchange of goods, the role of labor and business, and the functions of currencies. Education looks at knowledge transmission and also at the general ways learning shapes subjectivity and gives people an understanding of their social location. Linguistics analyzes the languages we speak, as well as the underlying ways that thought is subtly shaped in verbal and written expression. Psychology deals with the mind as a place where worlds are conceived in a normative sense and sometimes distorted by experience or physi-cal variances in the brain. Obviously, much of this book addresses factors that weigh on the mental images people make in the practice of worlding. Whether one is considering simple acts of imagination, fantasy, or the delusional worlds of mental illness, all forms of worlding are manifestations of human thought. Consciousness-altering drugs and alcohol must also be a part of any worlding discussion, whether the substances are used to bring a person back to a certain state of mind or enhance the ability to escape ordinary reality. New advances in imaging technology are enabling mental health professionals to use brain imag-ing to examine the underlying structure of the mind, as well as to track changes that occur over time.

World Philosophy

Philosophy figures prominently in worlding in addressing people's worldviews, or, more accurately, theories about the world on a grand scale. But to do justice to a discussion of worlding philosophies, an important concept needs acknowledgment: the privileged place of Western thought within a world of diverse views. No human culture exists without beliefs about existence, the place of the human subject, and the greater cosmos. Yet many of these beliefs have been ignored, discredited, or considered only as they relate to the Western mind. This absence of a genuine global consideration of human thought causes misunderstandings, intolerance, and conflict.

I employ the term "cosmology" in this discussion of worlding philosophies since it more specifically addresses humankind's attitudes toward the universe in both secular philosophy and religion. Broadly considered, worlding cosmologies encompass metaphysics (being in the world), epistemology (the nature of knowledge), aesthetics (perception and beauty), and theology (faith, spirituality, and God), as well as logic (mathematics and related topics), linguistics (origins and use of language), political philosophy (government and justice systems), and ethics (moral philosophy).

Given this laundry list of cosmological fields and the international scope implicit in worlding, can any generalizations be made about philosophy? The obvious answer would be no; there is simply too much variance in human thought to attempt any such task. But at the risk of oversimplification, a few cosmological propositions can be suggested. All world philosophies seek to map out relationships between people and their surrounding world or universe. Here lie the central questions of the human species: How is the subject (or self) situated in the greater world (or cosmos)? What is the relationship between the individual and everything else? Over the millennia, nearly every culture on earth has produced a set of answers to these questions.

But can we take this simple idea a step further? Consider how philosophies across the world have struggled with the tension between the human subject and the surrounding universe. In Western traditions, Plato, Descartes, Hegel, and Marx addressed this in their thinking about humankind's "estrangement" or "alienation" from the world.[10] As soon as our human ancestors became aware of their own being, they also recognized their essential difference from their surroundings. This much is evident from the first mark making and the origins of language: human existence is unique in the order of things. Christian, Islamic, and Judaic traditions resolve this tension by positing a God who oversees everything. Eastern philosophies often reconcile the gap between self and other in traditions describing the universe as one integrated system. The Indian Upanishads formulate an essential affinity between humans and the rest of reality. Ancient Chinese texts describe a fundamental "harmony" underlying the universe, as do the belief systems of indigenous cultures in Africa and the Americas.

Theology offers explanations for phenomena beyond the realm of immediate experience: origins of the universe, birth and death, forces of nature, probability of events, the future, and so on. Whether or not one "believes" in supernatural forces, a cosmic order, or one or more deities, humanity has, generally speaking, found such notions comforting. The majority of the world's population subscribes to one theological belief system or another. And as recent world events demonstrate, religious traditions continue to influence how people behave and even how nations choose to act. Hence, theology is crucial to worlding in both personal and social terms. Demographically speaking, of the world's 6.8 billion people, approximately 30 percent identify as Christian and 25 percent as Islamic. Hindus and the nonreligious account for 15 percent each, with an additional 7 percent of the world practicing Buddhism and 7 percent traditional Chinese faiths. With 14 million adherents, Judaism accounts for 0.2 percent of the world's population.[11]

Western Traditions

Keep in mind that philosophies generally build on one another as later thinkers modify or criticize the ideas of their predecessors. Some good ideas simply hold up over time, which explains the continued relevance of ancient philosophers like Plato (428–348 BCE) and Aristotle (384–322 BCE). Certainly, Plato's famous theory of forms retains enduring meaning in the context of this book's discussion of real and imaginary worlds. Plato asserts that what we perceive as reality is not the actual world but only an image or copy of the real, which we create in our minds. This fundamental principle has held great significance for contemporary thinkers, who similarly argue that people develop their understandings of life and society from "representations" of reality rather than from actual experience. Of additional significance to worlding, Plato describes at length the separation of the body and the soul, constituting a fundamental division between physical and mental worlds.

This dualistic view of separate corporeal and mental domains would take two important directions in Western philosophy, broadly conceived under the rubrics of theology and science. Western theology grew from the Abrahamic religions of Christianity, Judaism, and Islam. While these faiths would develop contentious relationships over time, it's worth remembering that they share common features, such as their human and geographical origins in the figure of Abraham and the city of Jerusalem and their monotheism (belief in one god), which contrasted with earlier Greek and Roman polytheism (believe in multiple gods). Since religion is arguably a product of the human mind, this turn to monotheism in what would later become the Western world's three primary religious traditions is highly significant to worlding in the way it consolidated belief in the figure of a singular supreme being. The Abrahamic faiths date to the millennia before and immediately following the establishment of calendars using the demarcation of CE (for "Common/Christian Era") and BCE ("before the Common/Christian Era"). During the Middle Ages, Thomas Aquinas (1225–1274) described the soul as a separate entity from the body. Aquinas asserted that the human soul has no physical matter or form and thus can never be destroyed. Belief in an eternal soul held obvious attractions in an age when people's lives were often cut short by disease or malnutrition.

The idea of a soul distinct from the body played an important role in helping future generations conceptualize the human mind. René Descartes (1596–1650) theorized a separation of consciousness from the body, observing that human bodies resembled machines in that both had moving parts and conformed to the laws of physics. In contrast to the body, Descartes saw the soul (or mind) as nonmoving and operating outside scientific laws. Immanuel Kant (1724–1804) identified the soul as the "I" in the strictest sense, arguing that this internal self is shaped by the material world but exists independently of it. To Kant, the ability to form independent judgments held great importance in allowing people to recognize timeless truths, or "ideals." Hence, the branch of philosophy called idealism was born. Kant and later idealists believed that we can be certain only about fundamental and eternal values, or ideals, because the world is essentially unstable and changing.

Idealist thinking was soon challenged during the Enlightenment by a new paradigm that would come to dominate Western thinking and continues to do so to the present day: realism. Whereas idealists desired timeless values and universal truths, realists embraced a world defined by change and diverse views. The Enlightenment Age of Reason revolutionized Western philosophy by giving people confidence that they could perceive, dissect, and ultimately understand the real world. As the dissemination of the printed word grew in the 1600s and

1700s, knowledge circulated at an accelerated pace. Science boomed with the belief that it was possible to study and explain rationally the human body, the world, forces of nature, and the universe. Here a divide would grow between spiritual idealists and secular realists.

Soon the mind/body divide consumed philosophical thought. Georg W. F. Hegel (1770–1831) gave great attention to the notion of the self and its perceptions. For Hegel, the self is defined through experiences of the world around it. (Subsequent theorists would elaborate this first-person process in the philosophical practice known as phenomenology.) Most notably, Hegel described human consciousness in a binary self/other relationship, in which the "self" confronts difference in the form of an external "other." Rather than a stable relationship, this difference creates a tension that the self struggles to resolve through a process of adaptation, which Hegel termed "sublation." Through adaptation the self incorporates aspects of the other into itself. Some have described sublation as the motor force of learning in that it represents the acquisition of previously foreign knowledge through argument, or what has been termed a "dialectic." From Plato to Hegel, Western thought embraced the pairing of ideas. And dualistic thinking persists to this day because it retains a value in organizing experience. Dualistic thinking is familiar and seemingly natural. But it is not the only way.

In the twentieth century, Enlightenment dualisms would be widely challenged but never displaced. Traditions of good versus evil in religion and the triumph of heroes over villains in storytelling continue to maintain a powerful grip on human consciousness because they offer simple and coherent explanations for experiences or challenges. When the United States found itself reeling from the events of 9/11, President George W. Bush famously described an "axis of evil" using such a dualistic worldview. "Either you are with us or against us," Bush proclaimed.[12] Yet, before very long, the inability of Bush's dualisms to adequately describe a complex world became increasingly apparent. Ever since the post–World War II era, philosophers have been seriously considering the limitations of such simple either/or dichotomies. These newer doctrines became most commonly articulated in the school of thought know as postmodernism. Technically speaking, postmodernism asked questions of Enlightenment-inspired modernism, which saw the world as knowable and evolving in a forward progression. Postmodernism looked at mistakes humanity had made, such as social prejudice and the horrors of war, and began to ask how people could follow destructive ways of thinking. Postmodernism asserted that blind beliefs in tradition and simple black-and-white thinking had gotten humanity into trouble. A more critical and self-examined approach was needed. In historical terms, postmodernism gained currency as civil rights movements were asserting the equality of previously disenfranchised groups like women, racial minorities, and homosexuals. The parallel movement of postcolonialism similarly emerged to challenge the presumed authority of some nations to dominate others in the world. Together postmodernism and postcolonialism continue to challenge conceptual views that would privilege any one authority over others.

Eastern Traditions

Early Indian and Chinese philosophical systems evolved simultaneously with those in ancient Greece (700–600 BCE); yet historical records seem to indicate no interplay or influence among these systems of thought. Hinduism and Buddhism originated in India, with both systems articulated in their respective dominant texts: the Upanishads in the case of Hinduism, the sayings of Buddha within Buddhism. Admittedly, both Hindu and Buddhist traditions entail complex and often contradictory belief systems. Yet, both Hinduism and Buddhism share a common view of transcendence regarding earthly existence. In Hinduism there is no single orthodoxy but instead an array of linked doctrines. The Upanishads set forth a program for understanding the cosmos and improving human consciousness by correcting misunderstandings about our role in the greater scheme of things. Somewhat like Plato's theory of forms, much of Hinduism proposes that our perception of physical reality (people, places, and things) is actually a world of illusion, termed "maya." The only true reality is constituted in Brahman, a state of cosmic being in which all things are unified with the universe.

The Upanishads propose that humankind needs to understand its role in the cosmos through an appreciation of "absolute reality" and "the soul." Hinduism famously describes an enduring soul that migrates from one body to another through death. The spirit's location in the particular body of a human or an animal is determined by the rules of dharma, which assign certain duties and obligations based on an infallible cosmic order. Over time, one's earthly behavior creates karma, which attaches to the soul and determines the spirit's future destinations. Westerners often attribute a certain fatalism to Indian belief systems, since earthly assignments in a given body are understood as matters of immutable fate. These Western assumptions often fail to recognize that while Hinduism suggests an acceptance of a particular location, improved reincarnations always remain possible with sufficient understanding of and adherence to cosmic principles. Yoga is a practice of unifying spirit and cosmos through meditation.

Buddhism derives from the teachings of Siddhartha Gautama (566–486 BCE). The many teachings of Buddha include the Four Noble Truths, the Eightfold Path, and nirvana. Salient themes are as follows: life's frustration and suffering, problems due to human craving and desire, redemption through meditation and rebirth, and ultimate enlightenment in nonexistence (nirvana). Most Buddhist practices include repeated invocations of the concept of no-self, which occurs with a recognition of the integrated unification of the universe. The concept of no-existence or no-self bears on this book's discussion of worlding in that it fuses real and imaginary worlds into one continuous whole.

In Chinese philosophy, Confucius (551–479 BCE) promoted tradition as a model for everyday life, emphasizing the importance of history and ethical behavior. Hence, ancestor worship and respect for elders figure prominently in Confucian doctrine. Arguments persist over whether Confucianism constitutes a religion, since it is relatively unconcerned with such spiritual matters as the nature of the soul. Confucius is known for his version of the Golden Rule: "Do not do to others what you do not want done to yourself." Lao Tzu's (dates unknown, sixth to the fourth century BCE) cosmology addressed broad concepts of the natural order, termed the "Dao," as the mystical source and ideal of all existence. Lao Tzu taught that people should seek to emulate the Dao and become one with the natural balance of the universe. Lao Tzu said that humans possess free will and so, when driven by personal desires, can stray from natural laws. Notably, Lao Tzu was wary of technology and its false renderings of progress.

Cosmology

Practically every philosophical or religious tradition projects a cosmological view of the universe and the role of humankind within it. Cosmologies range from practical theories about the world and planetary systems to more abstract conceptualizations of existence, God, and the universe. Often, cosmologies are maintained by scriptural teachings or religious dogma, frequently attributing the creation of the Earth and universe to a godly act. For obvious reasons, cosmologies influence how people conceptualize real and imaginary worlds, often in contradictory ways. For example, in contemporary US culture few people would dispute that astronauts have traveled to the moon and recent space probes have reached other planets. At the same time, studies show that most Americans also believe in the religious concept of a heaven or spiritual afterlife. In this way, it can be said that people hold in their minds simultaneous views of a material cosmos and a spiritual one. Recognizing these two views helps clarify world cosmological schools of thought, as well as the role of faith and religion in people's minds. Simply put, people often separate their ideas about the "real" world and their beliefs about spirituality.

Obviously, before the era of space travel people could only speculate about the physical properties of the universe. Nevertheless, early Babylonians, Greeks, and Hindus wrote of a "central fire," or sun, at the center of known space, and African and indigenous American cultures mapped out similar belief systems and methods for measuring time. Aristotle somehow quite accurately conceptualized the Earth as a sphere, surrounded by circular constellations of celestial bodies. In his *Cosmology,* Aristotle proposed that the Earth existed at the center of the universe, with all other heavenly bodies, including the sun and the moon, revolving in circles around it. This model would inform Abrahamic cosmologies of "Earth" and "heaven." For example, the Christian Church adapted Aristotle's vision of an Earth-centered universe in conceptualizing God, nature, and humankind. The church saw Earth as the center of the universe, as articulated in Old Testament biblical writings: "The lord set the earth on its foundations; it can never be moved" (Psalms 104:5). This religious view of an Earth-centered universe conflicted with scientific evidence put forth famously by astronomer Nicolas Copernicus and later by Galileo Galilei, who in the 1500s used a telescope to disprove the concept of an Earth-centered universe. But it was Isaac Newton who provided an explanation for how the universe actually held itself together in his theory of gravitational force published in his 1687 *Principia Mathematica*.[13] In more modern times, Albert Einstein would elaborate on principles of gravity, motion, light, and time in theories that eventually led to understandings of the universe as an expanding system rather than a static entity. Following World War II, during which German scientists had led the world in the development of rocket and missile technology, the Cold War between the Soviet Union and the United States provided the impetus for space exploration. The Soviets led the way with the launch of the first Sputnik orbiting satellite in 1957, a move that prompted widespread worries in the United States that such spacecraft could more effectively spy on the American military and eventually carry weapons.

But the United States followed Russia into space almost immediately, ultimately prevailing in the space race by landing on the moon within two decades.

These days, the role of the US federal government is declining in space exploration, as both foreign countries and private enterprises enter the arena. But in the final analysis, the exploration of space has importantly altered how we think about the relationship of our world to the universe, helping both to demystify our understandings of space and to recognize its infinite scale.

Utopia

Space exploration and interplanetary travel have advanced scientific knowledge and given humankind grounded insights into the nature of the universe. At the same time, the idea of exploring celestial worlds has provided new impetus for imagining other worlds. As a literary genre, science fiction can be dated to writings like Mary Shelley's *Frankenstein* (1818), Jules Verne's *From the Earth to the Moon* (1865), and H. G. Wells's *The Time Machine* (1895). Visions of a distant Edenic paradise thrown into crisis by human visitors now constitute a staple of utopian narrative. One of the most eloquent commentators on utopian thinking, Fredric Jameson, has pointed out that while utopias don't always appear as achievable, they nevertheless can serve an invaluable purpose in pointing out what is wrong with our current world.[14] This "negative" function, which throws the regrettable aspects of the "real" world into relief, dates to the famous *Utopia* of Thomas More, who gave the idea its name in 1516.[15] Historically, it's worth pointing out that More's *Utopia* emerged at the beginning of the great Enlightenment era, when many societies around the globe recognized that human beings were not subservient to nature and could organize themselves rationally and solve problems. More looked around himself and saw poverty, extreme wealth, and aristocratic class division. Hence, he envisioned an opposite universe, a "utopia," presaging ideas that would be articulated as socialism centuries later. To More, the "only path to the welfare of the public is the equal allocation of goods; and I doubt whether such equality can be maintained where every individual has his own property."[16] Indeed, in More's *Utopia,* "private property is utterly abolished," and citizens "contribute more to the common good than to themselves."[17]

While More's *Utopia* was a bit ahead of its time, it signaled the advent of a way of thinking about the world that would change how people viewed themselves, their neighbors, their jobs, and their families. Simply put, during the Enlightenment individuals and groups began to question their given places in society. They began to recognize that they could change their circumstances, move up or down the economic ladder, invent different forms of government, and even alter how they worshiped or practiced religion. Before long, revolutions were taking place, as popular movements overthrew the rule of kings and queens. Indeed, the Enlightenment shook the world by connecting people through print, travel, and commerce, causing an intellectual explosion that drove humanity into the modern age. And of course, this was a time when people began to imagine all kinds of new worlds. The exploration of the Americas was, after all, a journey to a new world. Let's not forget, either, that the great experiment that triggered the American Revolutionary War, the idea of a democracy in a new land, was a radical utopian vision that would reshape the Western world.

When communism and socialism finally came along in the 1800s and 1900s, they stirred up considerable excitement but ultimately gave utopianism a bad name. People are communal beings and willing to share, but only to a certain extent. So, an inherent tension exists between the individual or family and the greater society. Then there are the complexities of heterogeneous societies, where groups and individuals have varying needs and interests. All of this factors into the need for systems of power and control to make societies work—and that's where the trouble emerges. Most of the great communist movements of the twentieth century crumbled under their own weight. Many people date the fall of communism to 1989, with the collapse of regimes in Poland, Hungary, East Germany, Bulgaria, Czechoslovakia, and Romania. The 1990s and early 2000s saw the world celebrating the "triumph of democracy," in political terms, around the globe, even as inequities within and between democratic nations persisted. Owing to the persistence of inegalitarian conditions inside democracies like the United States (not to mention America's support of oppressive foreign regimes), few would say that we live in utopian times.

Taken together, the fall of communism and the disappointments of democracy have dampened enthusiasm for utopian thinking. And capitalism doesn't help matters. As a purveyor of its own array of utopian dreams, the tropes of capitalism—the American Dream, the Protestant work ethic, various Darwinian success stories—make all kinds of promises to those equipped to play the game. Unfortunately, the game of capitalism favors insiders. And as much as we try to fix it with social engineering, legislation, or moral argument, the competition remains rigged because a system that produces winners must also produce losers. Hence, the concept of capitalist utopia has largely become inverted in the public mind, as dystopian narratives of corporate greed and global devastation pervade the mediascape.

If you think about it, almost all movies about crime and success hinge on the drive for money. Hollywood has a long tradition of criticizing materialist impulses, from Charlie Chaplin's *Modern Times* (1936) and Orson Welles's *Citizen Kane* (1941) to recent television series like *Mad Men*. But direct critiques of capitalism hardly typify mainstream entertainment in a consumer culture so dedicated to free market ideals. More common are movies and TV shows addressing the consequences of greed and human excess. Stories about the destruction of the Earth are especially relevant to our discussion of worlding. Taken as a movie category, apocalyptic thrillers sell more tickets by far than any other kind of film. Practically all end-of-the-world movies make moral assertions about human proclivities. The genre dates to the Cold War years, when fears of communism and nuclear attack drove audiences to movies about alien invasion and global destruction, like *Invasion of the Body Snatchers* (1956) and *On the Beach* (1959). The first postapocalyptic movie was probably 1979's *Mad Max,* placing Mel Gibson in the role of a revenge-driven, motorcycle-riding, dystopian hero in an environmentally devastated Australia of the future. Of course, many of the most potent postapocalyptic films combine critiques of capitalism and world destruction, most famously those in the *Terminator* series.

What is one to make of the huge viewer appetite for dystopian thrillers? Obviously, the pyrotechnic spectacle so popular among moviegoers drives much of the demand. Not only do special effects–laden action films titillate younger audiences, but entertainment-industry moguls favor them because they translate well to foreign markets. Such movies feature little dialogue (the *Terminator* movies are notorious for this) and hence are easily packaged for non-English-speaking audiences, making Hollywood entertainment one of America's leading exports.

But could there be more to the nihilistic appeal of such fare? Might such entertainment satisfy a deeper zeitgeist in contemporary consciousness? A growing number of contemporary theorists believe that a generalized despair lurks in the public mind of the Western world, especially in the United States. What is one to expect after decades of disappointing elected officials, dubious military adventures, and revelations of corporate corruption, as well as a recent economic crisis triggered by greed and incompetence? Feelings of powerlessness and alienation run rampant in a society in which a creeping authoritarianism seems to tell citizens that their only means of expression or choice lies in consumerism.[18] What kind of worldview does such a situation engender? Certainly, for most people, politics has become simply another "world" one sees in the media—another half-real, half-fictional series of images that may or may not affect one's actual life. Alain Badiou speaks of the public's widening disappointment with politics as represented in the media, which is, after all, the main way most of us are conscious of our political world. To Badiou, many of us now harbor a personal view of the way we would like to see the world operate—a "metapolitics"—that is disconnected from official political representation.[19] But this metapolitics lies dormant, rarely addressed, waiting to be awakened.

At first glance, this seemingly free-floating disaffection might seem like a bad thing, a kind of groundless ambivalence and uncertainty. But dig a little deeper, and you recognize that the ambivalence comes from a distinct capacity for critical reasoning, a resistance to easy answers or hand-me-down solutions to problems. Most of us agree with the following truisms: life is complicated; we are bombarded by media; much of what we see in the world of images isn't real; truth is elusive. To put it simply, postmodern consciousness has gone mainstream. The question is, Where do we go with this view of worlding?

Some suggest that utopian thinking may be the answer, although different theorists approach the idea with different terminologies. If you read Giorgio Agamben, Alain Badiou, Judith Halberstam, José Esteban Muñoz, Chantal Mouffe, and even Jacques Rancière and Slavoj Žižek, you get this basic idea of a radical consciousness—a yearning for a "something else." Among all these thinkers there is an ongoing struggle to describe this sense of discomfort and dissatisfaction—and to theorize a way out of it. The vectors in the discussion have everything to do with worlding and the way one apprehends one's universe. But it is truly a multidimensional conversation—and a wild one at that—because half the participants would say that the conversation can never truly end.

To generalize crudely, we may be living in a moment of opportunity. Surrounded on all sides as we are by the omnipresent glory of "capitalist parliamentarianism," we nevertheless have Stephen Colbert, Bill Maher, and Jon Stewart.[20] *The Daily Show*'s ironic commentary about "serious" news programs uses media critique as a punch line. Critical insight makes us laugh. This can't be bad. Such brands of comedy popularize theory considered radically subversive just a couple of decades ago. After all, everyone is now aware of how media distort reality. But what if we still don't do anything? We have to look deeper. We must ask ourselves what makes us want to engage the world we inhabit. We need to take stock of the things that really matter to us, like family, home, friends, and a secure livelihood. Here is where we find motivation. In these worlds we actually make most of our decisions and do things that affect our lives. This is not to discount the civic or political realm but to point out that most big changes begin with small actions. Politics takes place at the breakfast table as well as in Congress.

What is agency? Where do we find the desire to reach out and touch the world around us? Sustenance becomes the object of desire that motivates an infant's act of reaching out. Secure attachment to parents or caregivers becomes the foundation for the young child's sense of well-being in the world—and agency (the ability to act in the world) can flourish or be thwarted. Securely attached children tend to engage other children and later become more empathetic. A poorly attached child can be ambivalent or avoidant, and the stage is set for a lifetime of stunted agency. While attachment is hardly the blueprint for adult life, it can affect attitudes toward authority that all children must learn to accommodate. Many educators emphasize the primacy of early schooling in shaping people's sense of identity in the world. Progressive educational principles stress "freedom," arguing that children should be encouraged to follow their own instincts and desires and that too much regulation diminishes both inquiry and agency. Traditional education historically favors "control"—or structure—in the view that children do not automatically know how to function in the world. Both progressive and traditional approaches can cause problems when taken to extremes. Too much progressive freedom can leave children anxious rather than happy. Excessive traditional discipline can produce frustration and resistance. Clearly, the nurturance of agency is a delicate balancing act. And this sense of self is put to the test as children negotiate family and peer relationships, not to mention institutional structures like schools, which often provide models (reward systems, for example) for occupational behavior.

The development of agency as a balancing act between freedom and control is important to understanding adult power relationships, especially in what we might call the "politics of everyday life." If we embrace equality among people as an important value, a recognition of the politics imbuing our most banal interactions as well as our government follows. The real trick lies in recognizing that we must simultaneously hold freedom and control in our minds as we negotiate the world. Aristotle identified this fundamental paradox in the citizen as the state of being caught between "the fact of ruling and the fact of being ruled."[21] Simple as it might sound, this contradictory position puts one in a perpetual spot of instability—a kind of netherworld of both struggle and possibility. The struggle comes from resistance to either absolute freedom or total control, but the possibility emerges from our capacity to simultaneously guide and participate in a collectivity. We should try to imagine ourselves both inside and outside these relationships and, by extension, all dualisms such as self/other and sameness/difference.[22]

Put another way, we might resist the seductions of simple oppositions that divide people. We might seek to "unlearn" the very ways of thinking that organize our opinions into either/or categories. Judith Halberstam suggests that the presumed rationality of readily visible answers may lead us astray. Maybe what we need isn't always right in front of us but instead requires a less official and more nuanced inquiry. Halberstam advocates a broadened and more inclusive approach to knowledge that incorporates both familiar and unfamiliar ways of thinking. This involves paying attention to alternative or devalued views—including an embrace of failure itself as an opportunity for insight.[23]

And here is where things get interesting—and I daresay a bit utopian. Could it be that the broad-based dissatisfaction with established political parties, the growing anger toward business-as-usual corporate agendas, the palpable resistance to authority of many kinds is evidence of some deeper yearning for change? Might a new utopian future lie dormant in the popular zeitgeist of alienation and disaffection? Certainly mass frustration is increasing, exacerbated by economic depression and cultural emptiness. Witness how easily the Tea Party and Occupy Wall Street movements managed to organize people looking for ways to explain their discomfort and dissatisfaction.

Let us cautiously consider utopianism as a possible answer. Needless to say, the dangers of utopian formulations, aside from their reputation as fantasy, lie in their narrow-mindedness when put into practice and their predilection for closure—dramatized tragically by, but by no means limited to, the failures of communist regimes. Still, utopianism might represent a response to the general yearning for a "something else" that contemporary existence seems to create. We know that much hasn't worked in the past. So we are not talking about something as simple as a slogan or a piece of legislation. It has to inhere in the hearts and minds of people. In other words, the utopian impulse comes from our core beliefs, desires, and understandings of our role in the world—real and imaginary. José Esteban Muñoz puts it well in *Cruising Utopia*, stating, "The here and now is a prison house. We must strive, in the face of the here and now's totalizing rendering of reality, to think and feel a *then and there*."[24]

As described above, one's sense of self begins with childhood experience but soon enters the realm of adult culture and society. Utopian imagination—the fashioning of better worlds—emerges from one's recognition of a need for change. While this insight might alter our thinking for the better, it has little impact until one decides to share one's vision with others, whether in the office, the classroom, the pages of books, or the arena of media. As culture shapes our identity, so we must shape the culture as best we can. This is a momentous time for such an endeavor. Even as Google and Yahoo! grapple with regulators to monetize the Internet, social networks and video capabilities are creating genuine possibilities. And this is hardly a passive phenomenon. Increasingly, the computer and game industries are recognizing the commercial potential of positive Internet applications.

The question that nags at cultural utopianism is whether images or ideas can change behavior. Certainly, on one level, much of what one does is influenced by received ideas. After all, the entire advertising industry rests on the premise that people respond to suggestion. But today many media scholars are skeptical about the ability of individual ads, movies, television shows, or computer games to have lasting effects on viewers. Most researchers agree that repetition is required to really affect people's thinking. In the 1990s, George Gerbner spoke about what he called the "cultivation effect," referring to the generalized impressions one gets from media messages over long periods.[25] Gerbner noted that gender stereotypes and materialism ran rampant in media and suggested that a latent brainwashing was taking place as people became accustomed to media images and began to accept their content as normal. But to Gerbner this wasn't a matter of direct deception. Rather than implanting ideas in our minds, advertising gains our interest by showing us what we already want to see, promising things we've always desired, or telling us stories we've enjoyed before.

Utopia Unbound

Early in the debates over new media, literary theorist Northrop Frye gave a series of lectures on the relationship of real to imaginary worlds.[26] Though they appeared in print nearly fifty years ago, Frye's lectures provide lasting insights into the character of utopian thinking. Frye asserts that we spend much of our time in a "real" world of everyday events—work, school, and home life—that pass through our consciousness in a continual flow. These encounters with the real world take place in the moment, demanding our immediate attention, but then immediately replace each other as time passes. The immediacy of real-world events leaves little opportunity to reflect or genuinely make sense of experience. To Frye, any broader understanding or analysis takes place in the more abstract realm of the imagination. Somewhat at a distance from the real world, imagination allows comparisons between everyday reality and non-everyday concepts of life we have garnered from stories and mythic narratives found in sources ranging from movies to classic literature.

This act of comparing the real to the imaginary is hardly a neutral process. Beginning in early childhood, we gather imaginary images of good and evil, success and failure—seeding our imagination with ideas about the kind of world we would like to inhabit. This world might differ from what exists at the moment. But, in one way or another, everyone possesses an imaginary vision of a utopia. If we have cultivated what Frye calls an "educated imagination" of rich and diverse mental images and stories, we can approach the real world with insight and criticality. In contrast to some media critics, Frye asserts that advertising gimmicks or political slogans do not easily trick us—if we have a suitably educated imagination. Frye took the issue of critical thinking a step further. Beyond simply arming us with a critical consciousness, the educated imagination provides an answer to the question of whether images and stories actually affect our lives. To Frye they do. The educated imagination is the very basis of consciousness from which actions emerge. The cultural universe of books, movies, TV shows, websites, and games can tell us how to act upon the real world—or change it.

This fundamental idea of a utopia in the mind of every person is certainly a romantic notion and not an especially original one. In one way or another philosophers throughout history, beginning well before Thomas More and his *Utopia*, have described idealized states of existence or imaginary worlds better than our own. But this very lack of originality gives evidence of the persistence of the idea. Clearly this utopian vision has gone by other names: the Garden of Eden, Atlantis, Erewon, Neverland, Shangri-la, Tao Hua Yuan, Walden. It all boils down to one simple idea, really: the search for a better place. One might almost say it is an instinctual desire. One might venture that even while recognizing all the false promises put before us, we nevertheless hold in our minds a space of possibility. The longing for a state of "something else" described earlier has been linked to philosophy, psychology, politics, scientific exploration, consumerism, media, and even schooling, among other things—all with legitimacy. Utopian consciousness is a truly interdisciplinary concept—and obviously tricky.

So can we bring our utopian imagination into the real world? Possibly. Certainly such a prospect must be approached with caution. First, let's acknowledge the preponderance of dystopian narratives in popular culture: the dramas, tragedies, and stories of destruction that entertain or function as cautionary tales. We see this in the literal dystopias presented in books rendered into films like *Fahrenheit 451* (1966) and *A Clockwork Orange* (1971), in genre classics like *Mad Max* (1979) and *Blade Runner* (1982), in more recent pictures like *The Hunger Games* (2012) and *Battleship* (2012), and even in kids' movies like *Escape from Planet Earth* (2012). Arguably, fear is the most powerful form of emotion in commercial entertainment, and it will be addressed later in this book. But for the moment, it's worth stating that darkness makes light visible: dystopian tales of a world gone wrong implicitly suggest what might be done to make things right.

But what about a more positive view of utopia? Dare we consider the possibility? This is where the two worlds discussed throughout this book meet. Utopia lies at the intersection of the imaginary and the real, creating an entirely different world. Most people believe that imaginary utopias are just that, imaginary, and can never be actualized. Similarly, most people believe that the real world can never be transformed in a truly utopian way. So we must think of something a bit new—a place where real and imaginary join, and the distinction disappears.

Let's be a bit more specific about what utopia might look like. The notion most of us hold in our hearts of a better place is useful, but what exactly does "better" mean? Many people would choose a place governed by two values: freedom and equality. Freedom can be defined negatively (as the absence of interference) or positively (as the presence of unfettered possibility). Either way, it is a familiar concept, except, as discussed earlier, we need to relinquish a bit of freedom to live with others. One exists in any organized society as both a ruler and a subject ruled.

What about equality? Really working toward equality takes some effort. Most of the world now lives in a political system called liberal democracy. The term "democracy" purportedly means that the political system provides freedom and equality to all citizens. But because liberal democracies operate in capitalistic economies, freedom and equality get distributed unevenly. And inequality is more than a matter of income disparity, as everyone knows. Gender, age, race, sexual orientation, geographical location, and level of education are but some of the factors that place some people ahead of others. Policies and regulations get put in place to try to correct the imbalances and hence give democracy its "liberal" inflection. But most critics of liberal democracy point out that this is always a cat-and-mouse game. As soon as one inequity seems fixed, another pops up. And every attempt at correction is fraught with disagreement between those who believe the system should be left alone and those wanting to fix it. So a kind of compromise evolves that always is a partial measure.

Legislation favored by one party or another passes through Congress. We cut taxes, regulate banks, change health care, and declare war. Worries about a divided America are no secret. In the wake of several evenly divided election campaigns and polls showing vast public disagreement on vital social issues, fears are arising that the "united states" are being riven by conflicting views on issues like gay marriage, immigration, and war. As a recent report from the Pew Center for the People and the Press put it, "The red states get redder and the blue states get bluer, and the political map of the United States takes on the coloration of the Civil War."[27] A lengthy debate on the subject has been taking place in American society for much of the past two decades.

Americans and people around the world are hungering for a new kind of politics. Traditional parties hand power back and forth in most of today's democracies, but the fundamental structures of governance and everyday life change little. Saying this does not mean that a radical revolution is in the offing or that liberal democracy is about to be undone. What is needed is something more fundamental and subtle, a way of changing people's minds, a democratic consciousness that will answer the desire for "something else" lingering in the minds of millions across the United States and much of the world. There is no single way of spreading this idea of democratic consciousness. But the method might be approximated by describing it as a form of education—or, more precisely, a form of cultural "pedagogy"—in which ideas seep into the public mind through conversations, books, observed actions, movies, and Internet applications.[28] As described by bell hooks in her formulation of revolutionary pedagogy, great power lies in the simple act of people sharing ideas with each other.[29] In the micropolitics of everyday life, dialogue fosters critical consciousness and plants the seeds of empowerment.

How does this critical consciousness play itself out? How is this yearning for "something else" satisfied? It is always tempting to jump on the bandwagon of a cause, arguing, for example, for free speech, the end of war, or the empowerment of the disenfranchised. These are worthy and necessary causes. But underlying all of them must be a more general understanding of the utopian possibility embedded in the "something else," or what Badiou calls "metapolitics." The problem with causes is that they temporarily blind one to other causes. Early feminist movements were famously criticized for failing to address race. Today's campaigns to eliminate world hunger can overlook the poverty a few blocks away. Often one needs to take a step back to see the entire picture. Inequities and abridgments of freedom abound in our lives. They are palpable as we sometimes feel ourselves reduced to lives of consumption and submission. But tempting as it is to blame capitalism or xenophobia, one needs to consider a broader view that is simultaneously more specific and more general.

How does one approach utopian possibility in the new millennium? The answer lies less in a partisan program and more in a frame of mind. The kind of politics that runs society—party politics with celebrity figureheads who repackage worn-out ideas—isn't going to provide a utopian reality. While we must recognize that utopia always functions more as a goal than as an achievable end, we might proceed anyway. As Jacques Rancière reminds us, power is not the mere exercise of authority "but a political relationship that allows one to think about the possibility of political subjectivity."[30]

A political subject resides inside each of us—in the self that allows us to act, and do, and make decisions, and have more consciousness. Once this politicized identity is activated and made visible, the stage is set—as is becoming apparent in today's widespread search for a "something else." There is a difference between the illusionary politics of the party and deeper visions of utopia that reside in people's hearts and minds. This subject can act upon the world—identifying sites of oppression, greed, and power gone wrong—and it can work in dialogue with others to change bad situations wherever they are found. This is where utopia can exist in the present world. It can be found in each person and in groups of people where imaginary and real worlds connect. And while it is a vision of possibility, it is now also a plan of action, in which conscious beings are ever alert and informed to confront inequality and injustice wherever they find it.

Utopian possibility requires a utopian subject. And the utopian subject requires knowledge. This is where humanity stands right now. Huge masses of people are dissatisfied with the lives they live. Some are mired in poverty and suffering; others simply find themselves hooked on consumerism and illusionary politics. The task for utopian thinkers is to devise a way of sharing a positive vision—at the lunch table, on the blog, at the ballot box, in the political demonstration—wherever the message can be articulated.[31] There is a path to that better place. The road lies in a utopian vision that does not need a name. Sometimes the answer may lie in simply saying no to existing options. In other instances one may need to proceed without a clearly defined goal or agenda. But inaction will no longer do. Reaching out, connecting with others, thinking the unthinkable—this is how to change the world. This is how the utopian imagination becomes real.

Notes

1. Jane McGonigal, *Reality Is Broken: Why Games Make Us Better and How They Can Change the World* (New York: Penguin, 2011).

2. E. D. Hirsch Jr., *Cultural Literacy: What Every American Needs to Know* (New York: Random House, 1989).

3. Henry Jenkins, *Convergence Culture: Where Old and New Media Collide* (New York: New York University Press, 2008).

4. "World," *American Heritage College Dictionary,* 4th ed. (New York: Houghton Mifflin Harcourt, 2010).

5. Gayatri Chakravorty Spivak, "Three Women's Texts and a Critique of Imperialism," *Critical Inquiry* 12, no. 1 (Autumn 1985): 235–261.

6. Robert Britt Smith, "Freeze, Fry, or Dry: How Long Has the Earth Got?," Space.com, February 25, 2000, www.space.com/scienceastronomy/solarsystem/death_of_earth_000224.html (accessed June 17, 2011).

7. "Earth," Wikipedia, http://en.wikipedia.org/wiki/Earth (accessed June 17, 2010).

8. "Food and Agriculture Organization of the United Nations," Wikipedia, http://en.wikipedia.org/wiki/FAO (accessed June 11, 2008).

9. Dale Allen Pfeiffer, "Eating Fossil Fuels," From the Wilderness, 2004, www.fromthewilderness.com/free/ww3/100303_eating_oil.html (accessed September 25, 2012).

10. David E. Cooper, *World Philosophies: An Historical Introduction* (Oxford and Cambridge: Blackwell, 1996), 5.

11. "Major Religions of the World Ranked by Adherents," Adherents.com, www.adherents.com/Religions_By_Adherents.html (accessed January 2, 2012).

12. "Bush State of the Union Address," Inside Politics, January 29, 2002, http://edition.cnn.com/2002/ALLPOLITICS/01/29/bush.speech.txt (accessed January 2, 2012).

13. Isaac Newton, *Principia Mathematica* (Cambridge: Cambridge University Press, [1687] 1910).

14. Fredric Jameson, *Archaeologies of the Future: The Desire Called Utopia and Other Science Fictions* (London and New York: Verso, 2005).

15. Thomas More, "Utopia/1516," in *Utopias,* ed. Richard Noble (Cambridge, MA: MIT Press, 2009), 22.

16. Ibid.

17. Ibid.

18. Giorgio Agamben, *Homo Sacer: Sovereign Power and Bare Life,* trans. Daniel Heller-Roazen (Stanford, CA: Stanford University Press, 1998); Henry Giroux, *Against the New Authoritarianism: Politics After Abu Ghraib* (Winnipeg: Arbeiter Ring, 2005).

19. Alain Badiou, *Metapolitics,* trans. Jason Baker (London and New York: Verso, 2005).

20. Ibid.

21. Jacques Rancière, "Ten Theses on Politics," *Theory and Event* 5, no. 3 (2001),

http://muse.jhu.edu/login?auth=0&type=summary&url=/journals/theory_and_ event/v005/5.3ranciere.html (accessed August 10, 2011).

22. Michel Foucault, *Power/Knowledge: Selected Interviews and Other Writings* (New York: Vintage, 1980).

23. Judith Halberstam, *The Queer Art of Failure* (Durham, NC: Duke University Press, 2011).

24. José Esteban Muñoz, *Cruising Utopia: The Then and There of Queer Futurity* (New York: New York University Press, 2009), 1.

25. George Gerbner, *Against the Mainstream: The Selected Works of George Gerbner* (New York: Peter Lang, 2002).

26. Northrop Frye, *The Educated Imagination* (Bloomington: Indiana University Press, 1964).

27. E. J. Dionne Jr., "One Nation Deeply Divided," *Washington Post,* November 7, 2003, A31.

28. David Trend, *Cultural Pedagogy: Art, Education, Politics* (New York: Bergin and Garvey, 1992).

29. Bell hooks, *Teaching Critical Thinking: Practical Wisdom* (New York: Routledge, 2010).

30. Rancière, "Ten Theses."

31. Paulo Freire, *Pedagogy of the Oppressed: 30th Anniversary Edition* (New York: Continuum, 2000).

CHAPTER THREE
CONSUMING DESIRES

Money brings real and virtual worlds together like nothing else. Itself little more than an imaginary marker for government wealth stored elsewhere, money is a product of mind on many levels. For most people, having cash in their pocket is about as real as anything gets. Money is the link to everything we need (or think we need)—so much so that many of us equate wealth with well-being, success, and even freedom itself. But at the end of the day, money is simply a symbol, a stand-in waiting to be exchanged for goods and services. Partly due to its imaginary character, money easily confuses people—whether we are talking about the investment bankers who caused the recent recession, college students racking up large balances on their credit cards, or the guy on the corner asking for spare change.

Money in real and virtual worlds tells us much about our beliefs and underlying ideologies. Money informs our actions and tells us what to do, lingering quietly in the background of much of the media we consume. Consciously or unconsciously, many of us spend a good portion of our time thinking about money, especially in difficult economic times. While many of our activities involve people (our friends, family, and communities), a great deal of our lives is directed at things: commodities like groceries and clothing, bigger purchases like cars and homes, and important services like education and health care. This chapter addresses our relationship to these goods and services, as well as the heated debates that have arisen around this seemingly simple topic.

Acquiring things we need or want involves a set of learned practices, attitudes, and relationships. Opinion diverges over the thought processes involved. The "official" view of democratic capitalism is rather straightforward. It says that people's needs are largely met by the marketplace, where goods are bought and sold—including people's labor—at prices set according to the laws of supply and demand. Better things are more desirable, which pushes up their prices, rewards their makers, and benefits society through quality improvements. Society is seen in this official view as generally fair; the system has no political implications. Hardworking people thrive and garner more resources, lazy people have less, and people are free to determine their own level of economic success or failure. Hence, natural processes of the "free market" regulate commodities and labor prices. Economist Adam Smith is often identified as among the first to articulate these free market principles. In the 1700s, as the world was moving from a mercantile economy (in which goods were bartered) to a capitalist one (in which profits on goods entered the equation), Smith developed a theory of value guided by what he termed the "invisible hand" of the market. Still advocated by many today, the invisible hand theory asserted that markets benefit society most when they are free and unregulated. Simple supply and demand take care of everything and everyone fairly.

The economic depression of the 1930s and the recent worldwide recession have disproved the invisible hand theory. When not sufficiently regulated, markets can start to accumulate huge profits and losses, excessively rewarding and punishing people as a consequence. Writing during the Great Depression, John Maynard Keynes argued that governments could keep economies from getting out of control. Without advocating complete federal management of the economy (as in a communist system), Keynes said that we could correct market problems with regulations, taxes, and incentives. The fundamental perspectives of Smith and Keynes are heard in most contemporary debates over government economic policy in the United States and around the world.

Capitalism and markets define a certain kind of mental economy in which goods and services are bought and sold. In fact, it's hard to imagine a "world" operating in any other way. This is one reason why imaginary and virtual computer worlds all adopt some form of currency for exchange. The point is that value for things (the amount things cost) is an imaginary idea expressed in some form of currency. According to Marxist criticisms of capitalism, this is where problems emerge. By buying carrots and selling them for more than was paid, a grocer alters the imaginary value of the carrots and gets to keep the profit, or "surplus value." The same thing happens when a business owner hires someone to make something and then sells the product for more than the labor cost. It sounds straightforward and innocent. But Marx believed there was a difference between the surplus value of carrots and the surplus value of labor. When workers get less money for their work than its actual value, and someone else makes a profit, they become alienated from their work and eventually from themselves. Experiencing work as a commodity to be bought and sold, people begin to see themselves as things similarly bought and sold. Over time people begin to focus on commodities at the expense of human relationships. The "world" we inhabit becomes one of objects and actions to be bought and sold.

Put another way, individual and group worldviews can be described as private and public. The idea of privatization has to do with the relationship between individuals and their communities. Most everyone agrees that being an individual can be a good thing. In fact, individualism is a necessary element in human development as a child grows into adulthood and establishes an identity as a person. But how far should individualism and private interests go? In a society that encourages consumption, competition, and individualism, ideals of community and the common good become devalued. The acquisition of things for one's own enjoyment can undermine values like compassion, sharing, and a better world for everyone. In Western societies, individualism emerged from the Enlightenment idea that people possessed the ability to make independent assessments of their world, without guidance from a monarch or church. Many Western philosophers posit the individual as distinct from the surrounding universe. Eastern religions, on the other hand, typically hold that people are inseparable from the universe. Individualism is deemphasized.

In historical terms, the United States was founded on the premise of individual political freedom. Democracy said that the views of individual citizens were more important than the governing rule of monarchy. In this way, the American system of government was born as a grand social experiment. Nothing like it had ever been attempted in the world on such a large scale. Many observers of the day didn't think it would work. And American democracy struggled into the 1800s with insurrections and eventually a civil war. I've written in *A Culture Divided: America's Struggle for Unity* about the history of disagreement in the United States and around the world.

The key issue is the tension between individuals and groups. How much authority should individuals and groups have, and how many resources should they control? If we need to accomplish things together as a society, how much do we rely on government to get these things done? Here is where people's political worlds collide. The US electorate is evenly divided between people who believe that individualism should guide our thinking and those who think more in terms of group interests—although most people stand somewhere in the middle. This is one reason why recent presidential elections have been so close, with both George W. Bush and Barack Obama winning by less than 5 percent of the ballot. It's also why so many hotly contested issues have been difficult to resolve in Congress.

On one side stand those who believe the individual to be the most important unit in social organization. Individuals acting in their own interests drive competition in the economy and politics. The less we interfere with the natural interests and behaviors of the individual, the better. Taxes shouldn't be handed over to the larger community because the individual has acquired money by good efforts that deserve reward. Government should be as small as possible because it often wastes money and tries to offer services that people should be allowed to select for themselves. The individualist impulse in politics generally coincides with conservative beliefs and the Republican Party platform. It also is favored by political independents and so-called Tea Party movements, named for the American revolutionaries who protested British rule. The individual-oriented camp generally supports capitalism as the natural expression of democracy and free choice.

On the other side stand those favoring group ideals. Group-oriented thinkers are concerned with the interests of everyone rather than of individuals. As viewed from this perspective, competition is counterproductive because it encourages selfishness and a lack of consideration for those lacking resources or abilities. Group orientation favors government as a way of getting things done for the community as a whole. Taxes are regarded as a fair way of sharing responsibility for things like roads, education, and armies. Group-oriented attitudes generally correspond with liberal ideals and the Democratic Party platform. In more extreme forms, group views favor collective forms of social organization like socialism or communism that trust government with taking care of people. The group-oriented perspective often criticizes capitalism as an unnatural force that subverts people's natural collective instincts.

The health insurance debates during the Obama administration brought into focus the philosophical divide that exists in the United States and around much of the globe regarding the role of the individual and the group. The individual-oriented side said the health insurance industry already provided care for people who had jobs or money and that the poor and disabled were covered sufficiently by existing programs. The group-oriented side argued that society should provide a government-regulated health care system for everyone, so that old, poor, and already sick people couldn't be pushed out. The debate highlighted one of the most important aspects of the divide between individual- and group-oriented perspectives: our attitudes toward other members of society. Are we simply a collection of individuals, as former British prime minister Margaret Thatcher once famously proclaimed?[1] Or are we a society that takes responsibility for everyone's needs, as Barack Obama asserted? While these questions are heard in political debates, they also play out over the breakfast table in every home.

People who inhabit worlds committed to individual interests are less likely to be concerned about others in need. Such thinking is encouraged by a commercial marketplace and mediascape emphasizing individual interests and things individuals can get. Think of all the ads for clothing, food, cosmetics, cars, and even careers, all focusing on what you can have, look like, or become. Emphasis is placed on the lone consumer. People are encouraged to think that Urban Outfitters, Apple, Heineken, and BMW are what really matters—that real happiness in life comes from having possessions. Of course, most people know that things in themselves don't make one happy. Studies have shown that when people are asked what they really care about, they respond that they value relationships, family, home, and economic security.[2] But the world of advertising tells us that the way to get these things is by owning commodities that make us attractive or better in some way.

While the impulse to own things and define one's world by possessions is hardly a new phenomenon, the process has progressively accelerated with the growing size and influence of corporations. If capitalism is a system of both economic rules and cultural beliefs, these ideals gain strength as corporations get bigger and more powerful. Hence capitalism influences more than consumer decisions about food and clothing. Increasingly it reaches us through the environments in which we move and live. To a greater and greater extent, people live in apartment complexes, condominiums, and gated communities conceived and developed by larger corporate entities. Shopping takes place less and less in heterogeneous urban areas or suburban avenues and more and more in planned shopping centers, malls, and redeveloped downtown districts. In the process, smaller businesses often disappear as regions give way to large corporate interests that organize them to maximize their efficiency and profitability. Think of how independent bookstores have largely disappeared from the commercial landscape over the past two decades with the growth of Barnes and Noble, Waldenbooks, and Amazon.com. The large chains have attempted to replicate the ambiance of small bookstores by implanting coffee shops and boutique-style displays within their store landscapes, but the products the stores actually place on their shelves have become less diverse and interesting. Malls and new commercial districts do the same thing, often wiping out small, independent businesses and replacing them with chain stores.

Getting and Spending

People make consumer decisions from the minute they get up in the morning and decide what to wear. While clearly influenced by media and social circumstances, these decisions also say a great deal about the people making them—expressing human desires, wants, and identities. Individualized decisions inform such everyday activities as preparing food, shopping at the mall, decorating one's room, tending a garden, or choosing a TV program to watch. These choices in everyday life emerge from creative impulses that live inside each of us—the expressive person who has been repressed by a society that teaches us that things like music and art are made only by the talented or the lucky. In reality, creative expression is something that everyone does. It describes who we are and helps us communicate with each other.

How does this process of everyday creativity work? Many people derive from the media and entertainment they consume an understanding of themselves as well as a pleasure in buying things as a way of expressing themselves. To some, consumer choice represents the use of a skill or an application of knowledge in the interest of efficiency, economy, or self-advancement. To others, consumption can serve as an antidote to feelings of powerlessness and alienation from big government, large corporations, and other institutions that exert power over them. The pleasure of organizing one's material possessions provides an expressive outlet that many of us take for granted. Selecting a DVD or the kind of car one drives affords a reassurance in expressing one's identity by taking a degree of control over the immediate world. Cultural theorist Paul Willis has written extensively about the expressive potential in the everyday pursuits of consumer behavior.[3] To Willis the "symbolic creativity" found in these mundane activities plays a central role in the way we engage the world, make sense of it through our interrelations, and stake out a territory we can call our own. Willis writes that "symbolic work and creativity mediate, and are simultaneously expanded and developed by, the uses, meanings, and effects of cultural commodities. Cultural commodities are catalyst, not product—a stage in, not the destination of, cultural affairs. Consumerism now has to be understood as an active, not passive, process."[4] Willis sees people's creative consumerism operating in opposition to a high cultural sphere he believes excludes most people. According to Willis,

> The institutions and practices, genres and terms of high art are currently categories of exclusions more than inclusions. They have no real connection to most people or their lives. They may encourage some artistic specializations, but they certainly discourage much wider and more general symbolic creativity. The official existence of arts in institutions seems to exhaust everything else of its artistic content. If some things count as "art," the rest must be "nonart." Because "art" is in the "art gallery," it can't therefore be anywhere else.[5]

According to Willis, young people in particular construct their personal worlds as acts of everyday creativity and consumer choice. He gives consumers a great deal of credit for being able to outsmart advertisers and retailers who work to manipulate tastes and control buying habits. In many ways, Willis's formulation of symbolic creativity parallels the beliefs most people hold about the market. Burger King, Pepsi, and The Gap may make convincing arguments about why you should buy their products, but at the end of the day each of us makes our decisions.

For all of its commonsense appeal, Willis's formulation has a number of flaws. The most obvious lies in the way it generalizes the workings of popular culture and high art. Consumption and the choice of a drink or a pair of jeans may allow people a degree of autonomy some of the time, but just as often consumers are responding to a promotional pitch they've heard. Michel de Certeau, among others, has commented about the indeterminacy of spectatorship and consumerism.[6] Individuals exert a degree of control over what they see and how they interpret it. They exercise some autonomy over what they buy and do with the goods they consume. But this control and autonomy are partial at best—and not necessarily progressive or even self-serving. As de Certeau writes, before we get too carried away with optimistic assumptions, any discussion of the way viewers derive pleasure in "the images broadcast by television (representation) and the time spent watching television (behavior) should be complimented by a study of what the consumer 'makes' or 'does' during this time and with these images. The same goes for the use of urban space, the products purchased in the supermarket, the stories and legends distributed by the newspapers, and so on."[7]

Wants versus Needs

So which is it? Do people exercise autonomy and free will in their consumer behavior, or are they tricked and controlled by the marketplace? After all, despite the choice and creativity that people exhibit in their consuming and viewing practices, doesn't the marketplace largely shape popular attitudes? Consumers may express themselves by the clothes they wear and the cars they drive, but most of the ideas and values they associate with those commodities generally come from the commercial sphere. Or do they? Can it really be concluded that the very image of a "self" that many people believe they are assembling by accumulating and displaying consumer goods is made up of images they have gotten from advertising? This raises the possibility that perhaps this image-constructed self—received from Old Navy, Nike, Puma, Guess, Banana Republic, Abercrombie and Fitch, Ralph Lauren, and Victoria's Secret, to name but a few—is really an illusion. Could it be that the thing we call the self is actually little more than a selection of images that we have been sold?

The answer is yes and no. On one hand, it might be argued that the presumed freedom we experience in selecting what we buy is really little more than an illusion of choice. The commercial marketplace has already chosen the array of goods available to us. It then simply lets us "choose" from what it has made available. On the other hand, one might argue that all of life is already a set of choices from what is available. Although we may be constructing our personal world from advertising images, it is a creative process nevertheless. Some postmodern theorists have asserted that there really is no such thing as an "authentic" self or even an authentic reality.[8] All the moments we experience are really little more than representations of a world because each of us understands those moments differently. Choosing a number of advertising images to represent us is just as creative and individual an act as naively believing we can experience reality.

Many people blame television for the dramatic influence that advertising exerts over us. Americans own more television sets than people in any other nation—nearly one set per person.[9] As Juliet B. Schor writes in *Born to Buy,* "Heavy viewing has resulted in historically unprecedented exposure to commercials. And ads have proliferated far beyond the television screen to virtually every social institution and type of public space, from museums and zoos, to college campuses and elementary school classrooms, restaurant bathrooms and menus, at the airport, even in the sky."[10] It is important to stress that commercials alone do not make people buy things. Most people begin to establish purchasing habits in the context of their family upbringing, learning consumer behavior as they grow up. Along the way, many of us develop a powerful drive to keep up with the consuming habits of our friends, neighbors, coworkers, and fellow students. There exists a strong social pressure to maintain levels of appearance and to achieve certain visible standards of living.

All of this contributes to a frequent confusion that people experience between the basic goods required for survival and comfort and the unnecessary commodities that people think they should have. Schor describes this as a confusion between what she terms "needs" and "wants." The fundamental items that people "need" are rather basic: food, clothing, shelter, and transportation. But most people are not satisfied with minimally satisfying these needs. Instead, a desire grows based on "wants": gourmet food, designer clothing, a larger apartment, and a fancy car. Schor stresses the fundamental distinction between what people need and what they want. "In the not very distant past, this dichotomy was not only well understood, but the basis of data collection and social policy. Need was a social concept with real force. All that's left now is an economy of desire."[11] Schor adds, "This is reflected in polling data. Just over 40 percent of adults earning $50,000 to $100,000 a year, and 27 percent of those earning more than $100,000, agree that 'I cannot afford to buy everything I really need.'"[12] One-third of the first group and 19 percent of those earning over $100,000 say that they spend all their money on the basic necessities of life.[13]

Consumer Society

For decades theorists have argued that people are persuaded to desire certain things or behave in certain ways by unscrupulous advertisers and promoters. In other words, they believe in a world driven by a huge propaganda system.[14] But that doesn't give people much credit for independent thinking, and it assumes that people's only real desires are those they are tricked into having. More recently, a new set of theories has come along that looks at things slightly differently. Perhaps ideology doesn't give people new ideas about what they want but instead caters to things people really value—like love, friendship, and safety—and convinces them that they can only get these things by behaving in certain ways or buying the right things.[15] This is the real genius of modern capitalism. It's gotten people to believe that the road to happiness lies in material possessions and superficial signs of success. This process of ideology makes the consuming part of identity work. You think you need to have the right car or the right clothes to look good and be admired. And who doesn't want to look good and be admired? There's nothing really wrong with it.

How did consumer demand for purchases get so out of control? Schor cites what she terms the escalating "work-and-speed" cycle. The American workweek has expanded at the same time that public demand for commodities has also grown. People work harder and longer, and they want more for their efforts. The cruel part of contemporary marketing is that it tells you that if you can't afford to buy those things, you're out of luck. And it doesn't stop with small things. Looking good evolved over time in response to the dominant groups in Western society and what those groups thought was important. In the United States, Britain, and much of Europe, this meant white or light-skinned people in societies governed by heterosexual men. If you look through fashion magazines—or any magazines for that matter—you'll see ads promoting a certain kind of beauty. It's a beauty of thin, clear-skinned, young, white women with enough money to buy clothes, makeup, and great hair. It's a beauty that leaves out anyone with a black or brown complexion, as well as any woman who is big, or poor, or over thirty. In this way the message sent out by the contemporary beauty and fashion industry is racist, classist, ageist, and degrading to anyone who doesn't fit its profile. And most women don't fit its profile.

Occasional efforts are made in the media industries to reverse these trends. *Marie Claire* editor Liz Jones tried launching initiatives to encourage magazine editors to feature a wider diversity of women, specifically calling for models of different physical proportions and more African American and Asian American women. The industry rejected her efforts, and Jones eventually resigned from *Marie Claire*, stating, "I had simply had enough of working in an industry that pretends to support women while it bombards them with impossible images of perfection day-after-day, undermining their self-confidence, their health, their hard-earned cash."[16]

The same basic rules apply to men. Here again stereotypes abound. Men are told that they need to look right. But with a man the emphasis is placed a little more on having an impressive car and other possessions that show he has enough money or is smart enough to get it. Media images of men these days often equate masculinity with being tough in certain ways as well. Here violence enters the picture. Many contemporary television shows, movies, and computer games tell a man that he needs to be able to use force and to fight when necessary and that fighting is a suitable way to solve problems or get things in certain situations.

This is one way that media violence really does shape people's thinking. It works in the background, in our subconscious minds, making subtle changes in our attitudes about the world and how we behave.

Attitudes toward Consumer Culture

Sorting out the complex and at times contradictory perspectives and theoretical approaches to mass media and consumer culture can be daunting. The three broad categories described below—celebration, condemnation, and critical use—draw together arguments from major viewpoints on various sides of the debates on these issues.

Celebration

The celebration view exalts the benefits of capitalism and the marketplace. It views consumer culture as a nonpolitical and humanistic enterprise characterized by a freedom of choice. The celebration view derives from the assumption that people are rational in their buying decisions and act in their own best interests. Juliet Schor describes this view as the "consumer-knows-best" perspective.[17] The celebration model also assumes that the marketplace reflects real social needs. The market satisfies the natural desires of consumers, who are regarded as well informed, knowledgeable about products, and in possession of accurate information about what they are buying. The entire consumption process is nondiscriminatory because it accurately responds to people's real needs without prejudice or inherent elitism. People make their buying choices as independent individuals, and these decisions have no secondary effects on other people. The consuming process is nonpolitical because it is neutral in value and because alternatives to the market exist and are freely available. Within the celebration view arguments are often made that people can patronize as they choose, shop elsewhere, or change the TV channel as expressions of their consumer freedom.

Condemnation

The condemnation view sees consumer culture as an expression of false consciousness. No freedom of choice exists because the overall range of existing choices is predetermined. A store may offer what appears to be a selection of twenty brands of deodorant, but the merchandiser has already selected those brands. The issue of freedom of choice is further problematized because some consumers do not act in their own best interest and at times make choices based on poor judgment or incomplete information. These poor decisions result from a system of marketing and advertising that promotes false consciousness by distorting needs and instilling irrational desires. Theorists of the Austrian Frankfurt School, like Theodor Adorno and Max Horkheimer, promoted the condemnation approach in the 1930s. This negative view of consuming was also a popular theme of the New Left among such US intellectuals as John Kenneth Galbraith, who asserted that people had been manipulated by an anti-intellectual culture of mass-produced entertainment and selfish values. Condemnation sees consumer culture as inherently discriminatory because it promotes unattainable levels of material accumulation and standards of appearance that are presented as natural and unchangeable. This view sees consumption as politically biased because it is often driven by competition, self-interest, and values of inequality.

Critical Use

The critical-use view is well summarized by what Schor terms the "new politics of consumption."[18] Consumers exercise the ability to accept, reject, or change when confronted with buying options. The ultimate criterion in making purchasing decisions shifts to determining what promotes a better standard of living—rather than the appearance of elevated status. Free choice is both present and contested as consumers decide whether to accept what is available or look elsewhere for what they want. Needs are seen as neither completely true nor completely false. Emphasis is placed on the "quality of life rather than the quantity of stuff."[19] The critical-use model confronts discrimination by recognizing that some goods are not available to all people and that certain consuming practices are destructive both to people and to the environment. Critical use is politically informed in that it addresses inequities in the availability of commodities and recognizes that some consuming practices promote social inequality by valuing luxury, scarcity, and unavailability and by working against resource management and environmental well-being.

These discussions of everyday culture, art, and consumption can leave one somewhat depressed—or, at the very least, perplexed. With so many forces exerting pressure on what we do and how we perceive the world, can any enjoyment remain in the simple routines of communication and consumption that make up so much of everyday living? The answer is yes. After all, one can't disengage from our market-oriented society even if one wants to do so. One can only make the best of it with critical decisions. But a posture of criticality can only be maintained part of the time. One of the tricky workings of ideology is its unconscious side. In my conscious mind, I may know that advertising and stylistic convention could be seducing me into wanting that new pair of shoes. But something deeper makes me want them anyway. The best I can do is to negotiate the dialectic of critical awareness and unconscious desire because both define who I am. A person who lives solely in either of those worlds is only half a person.

Shopping in Space

Consumer behavior doesn't occur in a vacuum. We make choices and define ourselves through our purchasing decisions in response to our needs and desires, but we are also influenced by outside stimuli. The entire advertising industry is based on this fact. Consider the worlds of shopping, in both real and virtual space. The designs of stores and shopping malls function to entice us, as do the endless catalogs that arrive in the mail and the growing use of Internet marketing to tempt us and track our browsing preferences.

Shopping environments in the physical world have come a long way. In *Window Shopping*, Anne Friedberg writes of some of the impulses that give us pleasure and motivate us to examine merchandise.[20] Friedberg discusses the powerful feelings that people developed during the Enlightenment era regarding vision. Entire representational systems grew around the simple premise that looking gave people power. Owning pictures of things gave people a sense of possessing the things themselves. None of this was a neutral business. Wealthy people could commission landscapes of their estates or portraits of loved ones and friends. Over time the gendered aspects of representation grew, as a male-dominated world began to develop conventions for gazing at women. Centuries ago, the visual character of many cultures began suggesting that women were in the world to be looked at. With advances in realistic painting and later with the birth of photography, the "male gaze" began to assert itself. Men would do the looking. Women would be the objects of their attention. And a kind of control began to grow.

To Friedberg, this left women with somewhat limited options. One activity that allowed women to gaze and speculate was consumption. Taking care of the home and their own appearance, women could "window shop" and buy things. So they did. Consumer culture offered a place where women were encouraged to make decisions, to express themselves—not unlike the way small children today find their identities through picking out toys. Now, this experience of being watched and shopping was not limited to women, just weighted a bit more in their direction. As culture became more visual, everyone recognized the desire to look and to feel the pleasure of considering ownership. In this way a culture of visual desire grew. With it grew a world of consumption.

Looking became linked to owning. In much of the world the design of urban spaces began to respond to this shift. Cities were designed to give people the freedom to view expansive vistas, to imagine destinations of great buildings and statuary—but also to shop. So was born the craft of specially designed shopping environments. This can be seen in the nineteenth-century design of cities like Paris and New York, with great avenues of stores. But as the world moved into the twentieth century and the automobile gave us mobility, consuming migrated to the suburbs. The mall was born in the post–World War II era—and the phenomenon soon flourished throughout the world.

I will discuss the concept of imaginary worlds rendered into commercial spaces later in this book. Suffice it to say in this context that malls differ from cites in that they are organized by the companies that own them. Hence, the disorganization, chaos, and heterogeneity of urban space can be minimized. Shopping centers and malls can become what Norman Klein terms "scripted spaces."[21] To Klein, "Scripted spaces are a walk-through or a click-through environment (a mall, a church, a casino, a theme park, a computer game). They are designed to emphasize the viewer's journey—the space between them—rather than the gimmicks on the wall. The audience walks *into* the story."[22]

So we are talking about a storybook world of consumption, a meeting of the real and the imaginary. The scripted space plays with the narratives in one's mind, lighting up received fictions and realities, as it appeals to our desire to travel and experience new worlds. In the next chapter, I detail one example of such a scripted space, a shopping environment recently built in California.

E-Commerce

It's no great insight that new technologies have been a boon to the business world. The financial world has undergone dramatic changes in the past two decades as transactions of all kinds have become digitized and networked. In this context the symbolic character of money as an abstract substance "representing" value has become further dematerialized by network technology. Banks collect, disburse, and exchange money through electronic means. So-called e-commerce is defined as the buying and selling of things over the Internet. The volume of electronic transactions has grown exponentially as the Internet has become a part of daily life, creating a new world of electronic funds transfers, online marketing, digital transaction processing, and various data-collection systems. Practically all e-commerce uses the Internet at some point in a transaction, although it also reaches into a wider range of technologies, including e-mail, texting, and mobile phone applications. While the majority of digital transactions are conducted entirely electronically, as is the case with access to online games or specialized Web content, electronic transactions for physical items show no signs of slowing down either. By necessity virtually all large businesses must now maintain a visible presence on the Internet.[23]

Few consumers today remember that commercial enterprise on the Internet was strictly prohibited until 1991. Although the Internet soon became popular worldwide, it took five years to introduce security protocols and high-speed DSL technology allowing continual connection to the Internet. By 2000, most large European and American businesses offered their services through the Web. Since then e-commerce has become a seemingly natural way for many people to do their shopping and banking. Amazon.com remains the dominant merchandiser of this kind. Headquartered in Seattle, Washington, it is America's largest online retailer, with nearly three times the Internet sales revenue of the runner-up, Staples.com. Launched on the Internet in 1995, Amazon was named by its founder, Jeff Bezos, after the world's largest river. Amazon's initial business plan was unusual in that the company did not expect a profit for four to five years.[24] The strategy proved quite effective nevertheless. Amazon struggled in its early years, even as other online companies grew at a quick pace. Despite some initial worries among shareholders, Amazon proved its sustainability during the dot-com collapse of the 1990s. While rival companies were going out of business, Amazon steadily began to prosper—announcing its first profit in 2001. Since then Internet retailing has proliferated at a blinding pace, led by entities like Staples, Apple, Walmart, and Netflix. In many ways the Internet has usurped the type of mail-order business once dominated by paper-catalog marketing.

Internet shopping and banking create their own worlds. On one level, e-commerce simply makes life easier. Amazon's initial focus on book, CD, and DVD sales expanded in the 2000s to encompass practically any commodity whatsoever, due in part to Amazon's seamless linkage to partner retailers. On Amazon one can now buy a baseball glove or a refrigerator as easily as a Dean Koontz novel. Amazon has also simplified the shopping and buying process with "one-click" purchasing that allows customers to skip any review of the transaction. In this and other ways, the need to read details or think about shopping is minimized—making the process easier and, many would say, more efficient. But the ease of Internet shopping also represents yet another way that reading and thinking are diminished in the digital era. Amazon and other e-commerce concerns have been quick to make shopping a largely visual experience, with pictures of products enticing customers and reducing the need to read labels or think as much as they might in a physical retail environment. This makes shopping more "fun" and potentially much more impulsive.

The Internet also makes buying things more personal and individualized. Unlike with shopping in a store, many people find themselves making online consumer decisions in the privacy of their homes on the even more private space of the computer screen. While some might argue that this isolation of the consumer lessens the influence of pushy salespeople and glitzy store displays, the intimacy of online shopping also capitalizes on the basic emotionalism of the consuming process. Here the sense of gratification—or even empowerment—stemming from Internet navigation and product purchasing intersect. Individuals often derive a sense of their ability to act upon the world from both these phenomena. Bringing together the Internet and shopping experiences holds the potential of heightening sensations of control and self-definition that many people crave in an era in which so much of life seems determined by outside forces.

Notes

1. Margaret Thatcher, as quoted in Douglas Keay, "Interview with Margaret Thatcher," *Women's Own*, October 31, 1987, 8–10.

2. Belinda Luscombe, "Do We Really Need $75,000 a Year to Be Happy?," *Time*, September 6, 2010, www.time.com/time/magazine/article/0,9171,2019628,00.html (accessed January 2, 2012).

3. Paul Willis, *Common Culture: Symbolic Work at Play in the Everyday Cultures of the Young* (Boulder, CO: Westview Press, 1992), 1.

4. Ibid., 18.

5. Ibid., 1.

6. Michel de Certeau, *The Practice of Everyday Life*, trans. Steven Randall (Berkeley: University of California Press, 1984).

7. Ibid., xii.

8. Juliet B. Schor, *Born to Buy* (New York: Scribner, 2004).

9. Ibid., 9.

10. Ibid.

11. Juliet B. Schor, "Towards a New Politics of Consumption," in *The Consumer Society Reader*, ed. Juliet B. Schor and Douglas B. Holt (New York: New Press, 2000), 459.

12. Ibid.

13. Ibid.

14. Louis Althusser, "Ideology and Ideological State Apparatuses," *Lenin and Philosophy and Other Essays* (New York: Monthly Review Press, 1971).

15. Hans Magnus Enzenberger, *Critical Essays* (New York: Continuum, 1982).

16. David Gauntlett, *Media, Gender, and Identity: An Introduction* (New York: Routledge, 2002), 195.

17. Juliet B. Schor, "The New Politics of Consumption: Why Americans Want So Much More Than They Need," *Boston Review* (Summer 1999), http://bostonreview.net/BR24.3/schor.html (accessed October 18, 2012).

18. Ibid.

19. Ibid., 15.

20. Anne Friedberg, *Window Shopping: Cinema and the Postmodern* (Berkeley: University of California Press, 1993).

21. Norman M. Klein, *The Vatican to Vegas: A History of Special Effects* (New York: New Press, 2004).

22. Ibid., 11.

23. "Electronic Commerce," Wikipedia, http://wikipedia.org/wiki/Electronic_commerce (accessed August 26, 2012).

24. "Amazon.com," Wikipedia, http://wikipedia.org/wiki/Amazon.com (accessed August 26, 2012).

Chapter Four
Mapping Media

We experience real and virtual worlds as territories. Worlds are places to explore, inhabit, or view from a distance. Yet, in the end, they are self-defined entities that surround and contain all that lies within them. Simple as this description sounds, the immersive character of worlds can make navigation difficult. And even this territorial model leaves out the important experiential dimension of time.[1] After all, the inability of early explorers to see "outside" their world led to the assumption that the Earth was flat. Maps drawn by ancient cartographers confirmed this erroneous view. As a consequence, early explorers lacked a sense of "territory." They didn't know where the *terra* ("land") began and where it ended.

Today a similar condition exists. While the shape of the Earth no longer mystifies humanity, more and more people feel lost and confused in real and imaginary worlds. Alienated from large institutions and their government, people hate their leaders yet never vote. Bombarded with media hype and advertising pitches, viewers distrust most of what they see while their familiarity with the actual declines. Meanwhile, Internet culture continues to supplant real-life interactions. Facebook grows as face-to-face contact dwindles.[2]

Communication Territories

This chapter on media mapping examines the demarcation between real and virtual territory, exploring it as a continuum rather than a clear boundary and making the case that the blurring of actual and imaginary is getting increasingly murky. In the new "deterritorialized" age of electronic living, we need a fresh set of maps.[3] In a way, Plato wrote about the problem of media mapping in his famous discussion of a cave in which those inside saw only shadows of what was outside. Prisoners trapped in the cave couldn't see the "real" world outside, so they had to make do with the "virtual" world of silhouettes. Plato was one of the first thinkers to write about the role of images in human society and to point out that such representations always produce inadequate copies of the world. Plato didn't say that images were useless or bad, simply that something always gets lost or changed in the process of translating the world into pictures.

Part of what gets lost is our three-dimensional perception of space. Drawings, paintings, photographs, and videos function much like maps in their rendering of territory. Images reduce the world around us to a set of marks on a two-dimensional surface that we know we do not inhabit. Plato's observations about the inadequacies of representation also tell us something about the way media and imaging technologies would evolve in the centuries to follow. The problem of paintings and sculptures attempting to copy the world as people saw it with their eyes would drive societies all around the world to work continually at ways to close the gap between the real and the copy. Tombs from ancient Chinese, Egyptian, Grecian, and Incan civilizations provide evidence of the powerful impulse to render reality in imagery. Over time, artists and scientists developed all kinds of methods to make their pictures seem more real—first focusing on smaller and smaller details, and later using lenses to project images onto paper or cloth that they could copy by hand.

Not surprisingly, the desire for pictures of landscapes drove many innovations in image making. People wanted to reproduce territory as something they could possess, or, as in the case of wealthy art patrons, they wanted visual proof of what they already possessed. It is now generally agreed that in the early 1440s Italian architect Filippo Brunelleschi created the first picture ever composed using the geometric laws of perspective. Understandings of perspective allowed Renaissance painters to achieve near-photographic realism in their meticulously detailed renderings of the physical world. As pictures became increasingly convincing, distinctions between real and imaginary started to blur.

This blurring increased dramatically with the evolution of photography, as means were developed in the mid-1800s to capture lens-derived images on metal, paper, and eventually transparent film. The rest of the story is history, more or less—technologies improved image quality, leading to the advent of moving pictures in the early 1900s and television by mid-century. It might be said that today's Dolby sound, 3-D cinema, computer effects, and even interactive gaming are but refinements in the long continuum of desire articulated by Plato to close the gap between the shadow and the real.

But the evolution of rendering reality in technological terms is only half the story. Plato was also concerned about the effect of copied reality on people's thinking, because copies always fail to be completely truthful. Something always gets left out or distorted in the shadow image, just as every photograph ends at the edge of the frame, and every media product is edited or manipulated in some way. This opens the door to authorship—to the image producer making decisions in rendering the scene or telling the story. With authorship comes intention, opinion, and ultimately ideology. The fact is that every picture we see, every story we hear, derives from a person or group making the media product for a purpose: to tell us something we need to know, to entertain us, to sell us a product, or to persuade us to vote or act in some way.

As photography was evolving as a means of communication, Karl Marx began writing about ways governments and industries manipulated people. Marx also saw that communication was changing how societies operated and organized themselves, influencing how people thought on a mass scale. Marx pointed out that this influence was being used to convince people that hard work would get them what they wanted, but the system was premised on an illusion. He called the illusion "false consciousness." Hard work might reward some people, but it couldn't give all people all the things they wanted. Systems of thought, termed "ideologies," had to exist to encourage people to tolerate inequality. Hence, Marx argued that the ideology of capitalism developed to tell people that having less was their own fault rather than the result of an organized plan. The American Dream version of this ideology promised that all could move up in a democratic society and become wealthy if they worked hard and played by society's rules. Of course, the American Dream relied on the fundamental premise that the rules were fair and all people had an equal chance in the game. It took generations of protest and struggle for US society to admit that women, minorities, and the poor were often set up to fail in the system because they really didn't have equal opportunities in education and the workplace. Such debates continue to this day in arguments that gay men, lesbians, and the transgendered, for example, still suffer overt discrimination and that many other groups still suffer from forms of bias like media stereotyping, which antidiscrimination laws do not address.

Media bias can be subtle. In an era when people often grow up with TV and computers, media-literacy skills allow viewers to recognize the most obvious forms of false consciousness, and news commentators from Rachel Maddow to Bill O'Reilly regularly point this out. Serious media criticism dates to the rise of movies and newspapers in the early decades of the twentieth century. European Frankfurt School scholars Max Horkheimer and Theodor Adorno, among others, described a communications system in which the masses were systematically duped into lives of servitude and consumption. To the Frankfurt School thinkers, cultural objects functioned as propaganda, and the citizenry was incapable of resisting the seduction of the dominant "culture industry." Although useful in the broad mapping of ideological persuasion, this totalizing position refused to grant makers or audiences any autonomy whatsoever. Unabashedly elitist in its views of "the masses," the resulting reflection theory, in its readings of media and culture, invariably predicted that people could be tricked.

Alternatives to reflection theory date to the 1940s, although until recently many were unknown to wide audiences. Some of these works emphasized the independent character of cultural practices, apart from the presumed overdetermination of the economic base. Others focused on audiences. Louis Althusser's work in particular sought to undo myths of unproblematized transmission and reception. In his paradigmatic essay "Ideology and Ideological State Apparatuses (Notes toward an Investigation)," he argued that subjectivity is socially inscribed in the relationships between individuals and organizations. Institutions like work, school, and media construct systems of meaning that put people in imaginary relations to the real situations in which they live.

More significantly, Althusser proposed a revision of reflection theory that put culture and media in a separate category from other institutions. No longer merely the advertising arm of a greater ideological system, culture was recognized as operating in a relationship with the market. In other words, a space was acknowledged between the institutions of capitalism and the consciousness of individuals. Within this space, resistances could form that were capable of destabilizing ruling power structures. These sentiments were echoed in the writings of Herbert Marcuse, who likewise argued against the classical Marxist doctrine that material relations alone were responsible for producing consciousness. Emphasizing the role of human agency, Marcuse said that "radical change in consciousness is the beginning, the first step in changing social existence: emergence of the new Subject."

These ideas were influenced by developments during the 1950s and 1960s in philosophy and particularly linguistic theory. Ferdinand de Saussure, among others, pointed out that communication was flexible and people had a lot more autonomy than was once thought. Earlier "structuralists" had sought to map out universal systems of how words and languages functioned. But while they did a good job of explaining how words attach meanings to things, the structuralists didn't account for cultural differences in communication or other factors that cause people to understand messages differently. The poststructuralist movement focused on the diversity and open-endedness of language, pointing out that people could misinterpret, ignore, or impose their own opinions on what they were told. This upset Marxist theories about false consciousness by saying that people could make up their own minds. But it didn't change the fact that people still could be manipulated without their knowledge.

A further refinement of Marxist cultural theory came in 1970 when Hans Magnus Enzenberger proposed in his "Constituents of a Theory of Media" that media scholars had been misguided in their understandings of how culture actually works. He suggested that instead of tricking the masses into a web of false desires, media actually found ways of satisfying real (but often unconscious) desires. Poststructuralists like Fredric Jameson and Roland Barthes, who further considered the negotiable possibilities of signification, later elaborated on this position. If cultural signs could be interpreted variously, their meanings assumed a "floating" character as individuals assigned them different readings. From an understanding of the contingency of meaning has evolved a complex discourse on the many forces that struggle to influence it. The very way one sees the world becomes a matter of strategy.

Technology and Immediacy

Technology extends human capacity, but it does so unevenly. Any discussion of technology's benefits must be tempered with the qualification that new things need to be purchased—and consequently are more available to those with resources or the good fortune of living where new technology is plentiful. Certainly the Internet has changed life in remarkable ways. During the past two decades, information technology has grown exponentially, and its effect on both the written word and visual imagery has been nothing short of astonishing. Envisioned in the Cold War era as an emergency communications network, the Internet was opened for commercial use in 1988. In the 1990s it evolved from a specialized tool for academics into a popular medium for everyone. Whereas the Internet was originally accessible to fewer than one hundred thousand computers, twenty years later the number of users worldwide had risen to 1 billion.[4] Dramatic as this sounds, it is important to recognize that Internet users represent less than 14 percent of the world's 6.8 billion people. With Internet access concentrated in the industrial world, a phenomenon termed the "digital divide" has resulted.

From a global perspective, the digital divide boils down to the simple fact of telephone access. Among prosperous nations, the number of people with landline phones, or what analysts term "teledensity," is substantial. For instance, in the United States there is an average of sixty-five telephone lines per one hundred people. Contrast this with countries like Afghanistan or Kenya, where more than one hundred people typically share a single phone line.[5] While South Africa has better phone service than any other African nation, 75 percent of schools have no telephone lines at all, and at some universities as many as one thousand people share a single wired connection. According to current estimates, such telephone-poor countries can't expect to match the teledensity of nations like Germany or Singapore for at least five decades.

All of this affects Internet access. The United Nations Development Program calculates that Americans have more computers than the rest of the world. In this regard, fifty-five countries account for all but 1 percent of global spending on information technology.[6] In overall economic terms, 20 percent of the world's wealthier countries produce 82 percent of goods made, with the bottom fifth making less than 1 percent. Ten telecommunications companies, like AT&T, Verizon, China Mobile, and Telecom India, control 86 percent of the phone and Internet market. This consolidated ownership carries dramatic implications for the flow of knowledge and values between wealthy and poor nations. It may surprise many people to know America's biggest exports are no longer weapons systems or Coca-Cola. Today the biggest moneymaker is entertainment—which is increasingly driven by the Internet. The enormity of the online economy often is said to help disseminate a "universal" medium in which human differences (for example, in nationality, ethnicity, or language) are minimized in one big global culture. But there is a huge problem with this optimistic belief, since the quite nonuniversal language of English (natively spoken by a mere 6 percent of the world's population) accounts for over 80 percent of Web communication.[7]

This blind spot about English is nothing new. Centuries ago the British Empire promoted the universality of English as it was suppressing indigenous languages and dialects throughout the world. This history involving English demonstrates how badly the assertion of any language or medium can go. Assertions of universality tend to obscure both the origins of a communicative form and the power dynamics attached to it. One can hardly argue that English was a neutral or innocent instrument of British colonialism. As with later visual languages like photography or film, the English projected an unacknowledged bias toward Western philosophies and systems of representation. The act of relegating diverse voices and ways of thinking to the solitary realm of universal language denies the multiplicity of a global society. For this reason, utopian rhetoric about a world unified by the Internet can similarly obscure our understandings of a world in which genuine differences and inequalities exist. That said, the Internet's English-language bias can't be blamed entirely on technology itself. As much as anything, the dominant role of English in commerce may be just as responsible. Moreover, network communications have indeed contributed to improved literacy rates worldwide, even as visual media compete with the printed word.

Most recently, mobile phone technologies have begun to take center stage in communications discussions. It's hard to believe that the first Earth-orbiting spacecraft was launched nearly six decades ago with the 1957 Soviet *Sputnik 1*. Cold War paranoia prompted the United States to launch *Explorer 1* the following year, fed by fears that space technology would permit enemy nations to collect intelligence from space—which they did. Thus began an era in which satellite images would become a tool of intelligence gathering, continuing today in international monitoring of aspiring nuclear powers. But commerce soon entered the satellite picture, as businesses, phone companies, and television broadcasters began using the technology.

With voice and imaging communications so widely available around the world, it is sometimes said that the need to read and write has diminished. And it certainly can be argued that the nature of letter writing and bill paying has changed in the digital age. Satellite-enabled cell phones now make voice communication more available than ever. Indeed, low-cost unlimited calling plans let people talk as much as they want. But, as any teenager knows, mobile voice communication isn't all there is.

Immediacy has always presented a problem for phone usage. Long ago, one had to get to a ringing landline phone to answer a call. Answering machines came on the scene in the 1980s to pick up missed calls. A decade later, cell phones started gaining popularity because people could carry the devices with them. Then texting allowed messaging to be captured and tracked in real time. And so we are back to the written word—albeit in a shortened and sometimes incomprehensibly coded form. Currently, over 70 percent of global phone owners send one or more texts every day. Alarmingly, 46 percent of teenagers report texting while driving their cars.[8]

The interface between reading and driving doesn't begin or end with phones. Global positioning satellite (GPS) technology for automobile navigation exploded in the early 2000s, with all major automobile manufacturers now offering GPS options on new cars. At first it seemed that companies like Garmin, Magellan, and TomTom would control the market forever. But the mobile phone industry had the last laugh, as hands-free applications like Apple's Siri eliminated the need for drivers to own a separate navigation device. Now car and phone companies compete with each other in perfecting ways to "talk" drivers though a sequence of directions. With an eye toward integrated communications, the General Motors OnStar system bundles four types of technology: cellular, voice recognition, GPS, and vehicle telemetry.[9] The OnStar cellular service is voice activated and hands-free, with a built-in microphone using the car's speakers. Some OnStar plans allow car owners to use the cellular service just as they would a regular cell phone plan. OnStar even lets its users surf the Internet, employing voice-to-text technology like that available with many smartphones.

For most people, buying a car is the biggest financial expenditure they will ever make aside from the purchase of a home. No wonder cars generate so much technological innovation. Some automobile manufacturers continue trying to attract buyers with claims of enhanced performance and safety. And they will always work to improve aspects of design and functionality with newfangled molding, upholstery, and finishing techniques. Further extending the reach of human sensory perception are sensor technologies measuring distances between cars and other objects or warning drivers about imminent collisions. For some time now, many cars have come equipped with video cameras for the same purposes.

But the use of sensor technology in automobiles seems pedestrian in comparison to what is happening in computer games. When the Nintendo Wii system came on the scene in 2006, its interface started a revolution. Unlike the button/toggle systems in the early Xbox and PlayStation controllers, the Wii responded to the movement of the controller itself. This represented a radical departure for gamers by introducing an element of physicality into game playing. Soon, the Wii had gamers waving their arms and crashing into nearby furniture to keep up with the game—so much so that Nintendo quickly assembled a *Wii Sports* platform to make the most of such play. Xbox manufacturer Microsoft responded to the success of the Wii with a further advance in sensor technology in its Kinect platform. Kinect enables users to control and interact with the Xbox 360 console without touching the device. The Kinect "natural user interface" simply responds to movements, gestures, or spoken commands from players—and has been an enormous success. Selling 8 million units in its first sixty days on the market, Kinect holds the Guinness World Record as "the fastest-selling consumer electronic device" in history.[10]

Growing Up with Media

We inhabit a different world than we did a century, a generation, or even a decade ago. But it would be a mistake to say that life is more complex today or that we have lost the "simple" pleasures of the past. Memory solidifies with the passage of time as details drift away. When I was growing up in the 1960s, most people knew a limited number of worlds. Like for a lot of kids, the most important for me were my home and family, with our cats and dogs. Then there was the neighborhood of other kids, baseball, and the corner store—an area of maybe four blocks on the west side of Bethlehem, Pennsylvania, which local residents fondly called "the Christmas City." Bethlehem also was a steel town, and the industry was booming in those years. So the city was another world I thought about, containing my dad's office, my grandmother's apartment, our church, and the end of the freeway that led to other places. And of course there was TV—all three channels—and my handful of favorite shows: *Popeye* cartoons when I was younger, then *Dennis the Menace, Lassie,* and *The Beverly Hillbillies.* By the 1970s the worlds I knew had gotten more complicated, as I'd started high school and developed bigger networks of friends, and the nightly news had brought the Vietnam War into our living room.

But those days were nothing like the world my own kids inhabit now. While our two children, my spouse, and I live in one modest Los Angeles home, our assorted cousins, aunts, uncles, and grandparents are located across the United States. We maintain our extended family world with phone calls and frequent flyer miles. Owing to the nature of educational resources in our area, our two children will each attend at least four K–12 schools, creating changing assortments of friends scattered throughout LA's eighty-seven municipalities, like Burbank and Beverly Hills, in a 10-million-person county of nearly five thousand square miles. This means spending up to an hour getting to playdates or school functions, as the automobile itself becomes a world to which my kids have adapted with iPods and audio books as well as conventional reading. It goes without saying that the Internet has had the most profound impact on the kinds of worlds children and adults now experience. First with e-mail and later through social-networking websites, we have all come to inhabit what writer Howard Rheingold termed "virtual communities."[11] Facebook and YouTube are the favorites in our house, although I use Twitter to keep up with conversations about current events. Significant in these virtual communities enabled by technology is users' capacity to shape and interact with the worlds they create. Never would I have imagined in my childhood the ability both to view and to produce videos about my life and interests the way kids do today. But social networking is but one factor in the more general rise in media literacy in the current generation, created by the exponential increase in TV-viewing options made possible by cable, satellite, and DVR technologies like TiVo, not to mention programming available on the Internet. Moreover, the ubiquity of digital technologies in current movie and television production has made possible special effects that create imaginary worlds in which the line between reality and fiction becomes invisible or irrelevant. The immersive experience of moviegoing has been advancing steadily with Dolby sound, digital projection, IMAX, and improved 3-D processes—all of which have enhanced dramatically the experience of theme park "worlds" as well.

And we haven't even touched on today's most important worlding technologies: games and mobile phones. These two media forms capitalize on the inordinately powerful experiential phenomenon of interactivity. Here lies the radical difference between the media of the last generation and those of the current one. For a long time radio and television functioned as one-directional experiences—and were roundly criticized for disempowering audiences by rendering them passive recipients of messages and ideologies. A counterargument to the passive-audience thesis proposed that audiences actually engaged media quite actively in their minds—choosing to accept, question, or even reject what they experienced. But neither side of the debate could foresee a situation in which viewers would inhabit the stories they watched by becoming characters or even authors themselves and thereby sharing a role in the outcomes of narratives. During the past decade PlayStation, Xbox, and home computer games like the popular *World of Warcraft* have permitted audiences to do just that by designing characters and assuming roles. Popular games like *Farmville, The Sims,* and *Spore* took the idea of imaginary worlding to new heights by allowing players to build their own environments in the game space.

Then there are cell phones. Technologists and business experts alike tell us that mobile communications will drive information technology and commerce in the next decade.[12] It's now a common occurrence during our family outings to realize that my twelve-year-old niece has become disengaged from us while determinedly texting her friends. "You're not with us. Come back," an irritated adult will exclaim in recognition that the cell phone quite dramatically allows one to inhabit the physical world with one's body and another world or community with one's mind. This ability to inhabit two simultaneous realities constitutes one of the most remarkable worlding potentials available to us. And texting is only the tip of the iceberg. Phones already deliver voice, text, movies, television, and games in their apparent progression to becoming universal personal computing/communications devices in the near future.

Nostalgia for the Simple Life

But hold on a minute. Old-fashioned telephones also let us occupy two realities at once. And people had rich imaginations before the age of high-tech special effects and immersive games. Travel from the here and now to imaginary worlds has always taken place in human experience, made possible by storytelling, pictures, and books. While the volume of cable channels, entertainment options, and new technologies has made more content more available in more ways, the fundamental elements of the human psyche haven't changed. People have always enjoyed traveling to different worlds in their minds, and throughout history they have devised contrivances to enable this. Another constant in human experience has been a habitual worry about every new medium invented to assist the worlding process, as well as an accompanying nostalgia for the somehow simpler or less threatening life of a prior time. In the 1600s the printing press threatened established political powers by enabling the dissemination of dissent. In the 1800s people feared that published accounts of crimes would encourage lawbreaking. With photography and movies worries arose that romantic entertainment would erode public morality. And today there are worries that video games will make kids stupid and violent.

In part these continual worries about the changes brought by new communications technologies stem from larger patterns of anxiety that have emerged with remarkable consistency throughout history and in nearly every culture in the world. While generalizing about human beings is a very tricky business, one finds in many philosophical traditions a fondness for a primordial past uncluttered by newfangled distractions. Some explain this as a tendency to look backward for a kind of refuge in a practice of willful forgetting about the ignorance and conflicts of ancestral societies. Others analyze the nostalgic impulse as a yearning for the unencumbered and protected worldview of childhood. Finally, our attraction to the past often evokes memories of home or a site of origin. Human beings are a migratory species. From the earliest journeys of Homo sapiens across the continents thousands of years ago, to the global immigration waves of the 1800s and 1900s, to the current movement of populations facilitated by modern transportation, as a people we often leave home for a better future. But we carry with us the memory of the place from which we came. And no matter how difficult that original home place might have been, it remains with us.

A similar uneasiness has accompanied every new communications medium in human history. As printing and trade helped religions and empires develop, worries also emerged about information flows, their political consequences, and the implications of materialism. The growth of print capitalism in the 1600s enabled the emergence of the secular state, as communication allowed populations to see themselves as citizens of nations defined by common ideas rather than physical boundaries. The marriage of capitalism and communication was hardly incidental. Technological advances in communication like photography, radio, film, and television marched forward hand in hand with their ability to sell products and themselves. Newfangled media and their commercial messages have enhanced the articulation of imaginary worlds in ways that have both delighted and horrified observers. Early printed tracts may have speeded the growth of public literacy, deepened religious experience, and disseminated news in novel ways, but they also allowed populations to indulge themselves as never before—and they continue to do so today.

In other words, throughout history concerns have arisen over the tendency of imaginary worlds to influence the real world of people and things. One can look at this through the systems in which imaginary and real worlds come together, namely, the products and institutions of commercial enterprise. Communication media and nation-states both rely on economics to grow. And the growth of one affects that of the other. The development of modern communications technologies has brought new ways of thinking and new ways of making money to many previously disadvantaged nations, while also enhancing our ability to know about events taking place around the world as soon as they happen. The broad-based dissemination of contemporary ideas and exposure to international markets has helped level the playing field in international commerce. As a consequence, during the past few decades, disparities between rich and poor nations have begun to decrease—and fewer people in the world now live in poverty than ever before. This is not to say that the world is approaching an end to poverty and misery, only to point out that, statistically speaking, things have shifted dramatically in a positive direction. As economic fortunes in the real world have shown a trend toward equalization, telecommunications and Internet technologies—not to mention satellite, TV, and other media—have gone global. The world is in a better position to share ideas and create integrated markets. It is increasingly difficult for any region or nation to be left out of the global conversation in the new, flat world.

The Flat World

Proponents of globalism often extol the benefits of a world of seamless markets, digital communication, and cultural homogeneity. A leading voice in this arena is Pulitzer Prize–winning journalist Thomas L. Friedman, whose noteworthy books include *The World Is Flat* (2007), *Hot, Flat, and Crowded* (2008), and *That Used to Be Us* (2011). Friedman has analyzed the effects of globalization in the areas of economics, technology, and culture.[13] He contends that, in economic terms, free market capitalism is the driving force of globalization. As markets expand in this way, they open national economies to trade and competition, becoming more efficient and dynamic in the process. Capitalism also contributes to deregulation and privatization in the global economy. Overall, the result is a transformation of the world from an assortment of isolated local economies into a single global marketplace. This yields greater efficiencies and a general expansion of economic activity worldwide. In overall terms, Friedman asserts, a century ago gross expenditures among nations totaled a few hundred million dollars with only a few countries involved. Now private capital accounts for more than $200 billion worldwide. "This new era of globalization, compared to the one before World War I, is turbocharged," Friedman writes.[14]

Technology plays a major role in globalization, manifested in advances in computerization, networking, satellite communications, and the Internet. Advances in communications and information technology have changed the world in radical ways. Following the separation and division that typified the Cold War era, globalization seems to be characterized by unity and integration. Geographical distances and physical boundaries once divided people. Now the Internet connects everyone, enabled in no small part by the falling cost of items like microchips and fiber-optic systems. These technologies make it possible for companies to situate research, production, and marketing in dispersed locations in different countries, while tying them together via computers and teleconferencing. Friedman further argues that because these new technologies are relatively cheap, nations everywhere can participate in the global marketplace.

Globalization has fostered huge cultural changes in the world. In Friedman's view, this has become manifest as formerly "backward" countries find themselves no longer cut off from the ideas and philosophies of the rest of the globe. Consider the effects of cable and satellite television, as well as the tremendous expansion of exports like CDs and DVDs. But it also results from the increased mobility of people from the farm to the city and from nation to nation. Never before has it been so feasible for populations to travel or migrate.

Globalization hasn't pleased everyone. Opponents of this "new world" say it contributes to the exploitation of workers and a devastation of the global ecosystem. The Alternatives Committee of the International Forum on Globalization has stated that while the "unrestricted movement of capital" builds up enormous profits for multinational corporations, it also creates considerable economic and social harm in many places.[15] From this perspective, growing trends like the concentration of corporate wealth and the diminishing ability of governments to regulate corporate behavior lessen, rather than enhance, the world's overall well-being. Add to this a tendency to prioritize profits over environmental concerns, the privatization of public services, and an overall erosion of "traditional powers and policies of democratic nation-states."[16] Put in concrete terms, those worried about the new global order point out that $3 T-shirts and bargain-priced electronics gobbled up by American consumers are available only because people in faraway countries are working for unlivable wages.

These concerns over the real-world consequences of globalization are matched by similar worries about the increasing commercialization of imaginary worlds. On one hand, the illusionistic capabilities of media have become ever more potent. From photography to television to 3-D movies with Dolby sound, the ability of media to provide virtual experience has grown—both expanding and replacing human abilities to render imaginary scenarios. As illusionistic capacities have grown, so have the interactive aspects of media. In reading and viewing visual media, we interact with a story by imagining it in our minds. But with games and the Internet, this interactive experience becomes more visceral. We psychically enter the world of an entertainment product or online community. As those worlds respond and change based on our actions, we become ever more engaged in and stimulated by the experience.

Representation and Storytelling

Reading and other visual media operate by telling stories. Aristotle outlined the basic mechanics of storytelling in his *Poetics,* describing a set of principles for an "ideal narrative."[17] Most obviously to Aristotle, a story needs a plot with a clearly recognizable beginning, middle, and end. He asserted that a tension was necessary in the middle of the story to engage people and keep them interested in what would happen next. In Aristotle's classical formulation the tension would emerge from a conflict facing a central figure, or "hero," which would generate sympathy or fear in the audience. Ultimately the story should conclude with a resolution of the conflict, producing a catharsis (a mental cleansing) in the audience from which some new understanding would emerge.

One can recognize this fundamental Aristotelian model of storytelling in all media. Yet it's important to remember that Aristotle formulated his ideas in an era in which stories were only told in spoken or written formats. The linear model of storytelling is a product of an age when people communicated with one idea following another in a sequence. Pictures and sculptures existed, of course. But they generally were quite simple in comparison to images today, focusing—as in Aristotle's formulation of stories—on singular heroes or well-known events. The emergence of the photograph radically changed the way people communicated, suddenly presenting lots of information and detail in a single frame—which got even more complex as moving pictures and then movies with sound became available.

It's hard to ignore the reality that movies, TV, and the Internet have become the great storytellers in today's world. Media surround us like the air we breathe. Given the ubiquity of media, many analysts now argue that television, movies, and computer media have assumed a primary role as educators in contemporary society. So much of what we know and believe about the world comes from the screen; it's time to acknowledge that such storytelling should be taken very seriously.

From a progressive educational perspective, there is nothing wrong with learning from popular culture. Writing in the 1920s, educational theorist John Dewey argued that a child's native curiosity and personal experience in exploring the world are much more important than a socially constructed and hierarchical system of learning. The ideas of progressive education were taken up with great enthusiasm in the post–World War II explosion in television and movies. Amid fears that media consumption was simply "too easy" a form of garnering knowledge, progressives argued that fighting popular culture was a losing battle. The belief in media as teacher was perhaps no more stridently advocated than by Canadian theorist Marshall McLuhan, who suggested in 1966, "The time is coming, if it is not already here, when children can learn far more, far faster in the outside world than within schoolhouse walls."[18]

Taking up the cause in the 1980s, progressive educators pointed to the emerging dichotomy between school knowledge and student-driven learning taking place in their homes. Most were careful not to condemn the school experience unequivocally and rather to argue that experience outside school should be embraced as a useful supplement in educating the whole child. As stated by Henry A. Giroux, "This is not an argument against providing students with what some have called the 'Great Books' or any romantic celebration of popular culture" but instead a call to "expand rather than limit the potentialities that various students have to be literate."[19]

What drives the lure of visual media as a storytelling device? Perhaps the most compelling factor in historical terms is the human desire for "realism," our fascination with images that somehow replicate lived experience and serve it up for the spectator's observation. Three factors come into play: memory, storytelling, and power. Early cave paintings captivated their makers by rendering experience in pictorial form. Anthropologists believe that prehistoric images of hunting excursions were scrawled on rock walls as a quasi-religious means of recalling a successful hunt so that it could be replicated.[20] Early mark makers wanted a way of remembering important events so that they could hold on to them. Memories are ephemeral and fleeting, but an image can help bring back a moment so that it can be shared with others. We see this concept of memory in later image making. During medieval and Renaissance times, the desire rose to illustrate and historicize everything society saw as important. Religion and property figure prominently. From cemetery inscriptions to portraits of the powerful and their possessions, sculpture and painting rendered mental impressions in material form. In times when human life itself was short and fragile, the permanence of stone and paint provided an obvious source of comfort.

During the Enlightenment era, science brought innovations in the ways people could make copies of their world. In the 1400s Italian architect Filippo Brunelleschi recognized that our eyes triangulate distance as we gaze on a scene. Like many artists of the time, he had pondered how to make drawings of buildings look "real." He recognized that as a person stares at a distant building, the contours of the structure appear to converge at a single distant point. Terming this optical effect "one-point" perspective, Brunelleschi mapped out a system for applying it in making images. This important discovery remains a key principle taught in drawing courses today.

But the impulse to replicate nature in visual form had been following another course that would prove to be of even greater significance. This involved the making of what we might call an artificial eye. By some accounts it all happened by accident—a tiny hole in the wall of a darkened room projected an inverted image of the outside world. Mentions of such unexplained optical effects appear in early Chinese and Greek literature. But however it started, the fundamental phenomena of pinhole optics were enhanced during the Enlightenment with lenses and mirrors. The "camera obscura" became enormously popular as a curiosity and an aid to artists and portraitists well before the invention of photography. Leonardo Da Vinci, among others, used the camera obscura to study geometry and physics. By the 1800s, painters like Jan Vermeer were using similar devices to create hand-painted landscapes that seemed nearly photographic in their detail.

So lens-derived pictures existed well before the advent of the chemistry that would make photography possible. In historical terms, photography seems a perfect example of a technology waiting to happen. People everywhere were looking for detailed images in perfect perspective. The problem was that such pictures had to be made laboriously by hand. Finally, Johan Schulze noticed in 1725 that the sun would darken silver salts, and in short order Louis Daguerre and Henry Fox Talbot applied these principles in techniques for fixing images on sheets of chemically coated paper or metal. By the mid-1800s photography had been born. Of course, "the mirror with a memory" was a terribly cumbersome affair in its early years—requiring wet chemical preparations in complete darkness. Nevertheless, the public's powerful hunger for photographic realism greeted the awkward technology with enormous enthusiasm.

Initially, the art of photography was so complicated that only professionals could practice it. People yearned for the ability to make their own photographs. In 1874, George Eastman decided to take on the task of making photography more accessible. After several years of experimentation with gelatin emulsions, Eastman came up with his Kodak dry-plate process, which he patented in both Britain and the United States. The "snapshot" soon became a sensation, with the marketing slogan, "You press the button, we do the rest." Without exaggeration, it can be said that Eastman single-handedly brought photography into everyday life. Suddenly, anyone could take birthday pictures and record vacations.

At the same time, photography was finding its way into print. Replacing hand-rendered engravings, news photography came into use through images of armed conflict. Photographs of the Crimean War began circulating in Europe during the 1850s, but the photojournalism associated with the American Civil War brought the realities of human conflict to the public as never before.

Keep in mind that in these early years society had not yet reckoned with the notion that a photograph might be something other than a "true" copy of reality. History remembers Mathew Brady as one of the great documentarians of the nineteenth century, largely based on his portraits of Civil War soldiers and battlefield dead. Less known are the scandals surrounding Brady's manipulation of battlefield scenes to intensify their dramatic appeal. Specifically, Brady's photographic crew arranged the bodies of Confederate dead after the Battle of Gettysburg to improve pictures later to be published. It's important to see this apparent deception in historical context. As with most portraitists of the time, the Brady Studio had routinely arranged and dressed up customers to present them in the best possible way. Meanwhile, other photographers, like Henry Peach Robinson, had begun using photomontage to assemble single images of people into group portraits. In the 1860s no one had much reason to question photography's assumed objectivity. After all, all previous "journalistic" rendering had been sketched by hand or drawn from memory. With the invention of photography, people naturally expected that a "mechanically" made image removed the human hand from the equation.

For many years most people believed that "the camera never lies." Photographs became a mainstay of journalistic objectivity and would be used as legal evidence. This naive faith in mechanical "realism" couldn't last forever. As the medium's novelty wore off, the public eventually lost its awe of photography. This occurred as the presence of images became ubiquitous in everyday life. Of course, some level of suspicion about mass-produced "information" had been present throughout the nineteenth century. People knew full well that advertisers and politicians had their own interests at heart. But as populations began to aggregate in industrial cities in the early 1900s, the production and marketing of commodities of all kinds grew—and emergent urban populations hungered for information and entertainment. Photographic publishing and motion picture technologies improved as their audiences continued to grow. In the years leading up to America's Great Depression, media had become a staple of daily life.

The Media Entertainment Complex

No one could have predicted that by the end of the twentieth century media would become America's leading industry. The consistent growth of the nation's film and television industries would transform the United States from an industrial producer to an information economy. By 1930 over 80 million people were going to the movies every week. Audiences were seeking comfortable yet novel spaces that could temporarily remove them from the routines of daily life. Movie theater impresarios like Sid Grauman in Los Angeles and S. L. "Roxy" Rothapfel in New York opened opulent theaters with attention-getting names like the Egyptian, the Metropolitan, and the Chinese.[21] Aside from simply providing entertainment, these new movie houses served an important social function in America's emerging metropolitan centers. By going to movies people became audiences, but they also recognized themselves as members of communities. Some have argued that the sense of identity and belonging that came from moviegoing had specific ideological overtones. To Ella Shohat and Robert Stam, "The cinema's institutional ritual of gathering a community—spectators who share a region, language, and culture—homologizes, in a sense, the symbolic gathering of the nation."[22] While it would be a mistake to overly politicize the effects of cinematic spectatorship, one can't deny what a huge social phenomenon movies had become. It has even been argued that this new form of mass entertainment pacified the public in a time of economic uncertainty, diverting attention from the mounting gap between rich and poor and giving people comfort as members of a single national family.[23]

Soon intellectuals began to express concerns about the effects of popular entertainment. Criticisms of capitalism drawn from the works of Karl Marx and Friedrich Engels gained potency as the new consumer culture grew. In the 1930s and 1940s, Marxist figures in the Frankfurt School would begin to describe what they perceived as the "manipulation" of the "masses." Notably, Max Horkheimer and Theodor Adorno wrote that audiences were powerless to resist the seductive allure of consumption.[24] According to this argument, people became ensnared unknowingly in an endless cycle of working and spending. Frankfurt School scholars would argue that the mass media played an enormous, yet surreptitious, role in convincing people to accept their circumstances without question.

These critiques of American capitalism went mainstream during the Great Depression of the 1930s, as Hollywood took up the cause in the name of ordinary citizens. Influenced by leftist theater groups in New York City, Depression-era films dramatized conflicts between individual and collective values. Major studios like Warner Bros. hired East Coast writers with a political ax to grind on issues like poverty and crime. Often drawing on newspaper headlines of the day, Paramount Studios made a name for itself with gangster movies like *Little*

Caesar (1931) and *The Public Enemy* (1931). These films typically portrayed young men and women forced into crime by a society obsessed with material gain. In addition to films featuring crime and violence, this era also witnessed a huge output of entertainment about the unscrupulous behavior of the rich and powerful. Ironically, these movies about the evils of capitalism didn't have much effect on people's desire to get ahead or accumulate as much as possible.

It's no secret that today mass media have taken over public life. According to the latest Time Use Survey from the US Department of Labor, Americans over fifteen spend 60 percent of their leisure time in front of TVs and computers—leaving less than two hours per day for such things as socializing, reading, exercising, and thinking.[25] Although one might expect that people spend most of their time online, 90 percent of the average American's time spent with media still goes to watching television. There have been many attempts to explain television's ability to attract and hold an audience's attention. Put simply, people seem to find TV more interesting than other activities. The medium fashions a world of engaging stories and stimulating imagery—but, of course, it does more than that.

For most people, watching TV doesn't require much effort. In the past decade the number of TVs in a typical American home has risen to two, regardless of family income. In fact, more families own a color set than own a washing machine.[26] Despite the increasing amount of time people spend with computers or phones, televisions are playing in the average American home nearly seven hours per day.[27] The relentless demand for television has kept the price of TV sets on a continual decline, and television is now a central feature of every home environment. TV viewing has become naturalized and destigmatized. Popular criticisms of TV as "mind candy" or "a vast wasteland," as an FCC chairman once declared, have all but disappeared.[28] Instead, television is now regarded as a cultural necessity and a vital resource for news and information.

Let's face it: many people get most of what they know about the "world" from television. A lot of us will never travel to another country or even visit parts of our own communities. This doesn't have to be a bad thing. TV can take us places we can't physically go to and introduce us to people we might never meet. The medium can teach us important lessons about those different from ourselves. In this way television holds the potential to promote human understanding, build tolerance, and perhaps head off conflicts before they get out of control. But there's one big problem. We always have to keep in mind that television is never a fair and unbiased conveyer of information. By necessity, mass media offer us a highly selective view of the world. Due to the economic imperatives of attracting large audiences, TV and related media do not present a "real" image of the world—certainly not an image of the world that resembles the lives of viewers. This is because for most of us, our "real" lives are not peppered with car chases, murder plots, and torrid love affairs. To put it bluntly, real life tends to be rather boring. So to entertain us television offers an exaggerated image of existence, designed specifically to capture and hold audience attention.

Commerce is the engine behind television's relentless artificiality. Programs are paid for by companies with things to sell. The shows most people watch are tremendously costly productions that can only be financed by advertisers wanting access to the gigantic audiences that TV reaches. While TV might seem a commonplace and ordinary part of American culture, in reality TV production is a highly selective and competitive affair. Broadcasting executives relentlessly search for programs designed to capture viewers quickly, lining them up for commercial pitches. The fierce competition for audiences eliminates anything that can't promise guaranteed results. This is why most television looks the same. It seems that in the interest of reaching ever-larger markets, television is compelled to limit its offerings to an ever-smaller range of stories.

Global Media Industries

Everyone knows that media corporations are now huge. The ongoing consolidation of communications, entertainment, and publishing entities and their acquisition by mammoth transnational corporations has translated into operating philosophies and business procedures quite different from those of the movie studios, networks, and publishers of the past. Gone are the days of powerful movie moguls making individual decisions based on their own creative instincts or personal tastes. The same holds true for television, where visionary network executives once called the shots and stood behind risky dramatic series, edgy comedies, and fearless news departments. Publishing likewise is now a brutal numbers game, with small presses and independent bookstores giving way to huge media conglomerates and Amazon.com. These changes in the way media operate result from a pattern of corporate mergers and acquisitions that began accelerating two decades ago. In some areas the process began even earlier, as Hollywood studios, radio networks, and publishing entities began merging and buying one another in the decade following World War II.

Why does any of this matter? While we can lament the lack of diversity and the shrinking number of voices receiving exposure, the most serious concern has to do with the purpose of communication itself. Innovation and creativity are no longer the currencies driving movies, television, and publishing. The colossal multimedia empires and gigantic corporations that have swallowed once discrete media companies have no intrinsic interest in movies or television or news, but they have a huge interest—one that translates into an all-consuming mandate—in generating profits. The many thousands of shareholders who "own" these corporations simply want a reasonable return on their investments. And we are not simply speaking of Wall Street fat cats here. The megacorporations responsible for transforming the mediascape must answer to small investors as well as large ones, retirees as well as hedge fund managers. The bottom line is that money—not ethics, or taste, or politics—is now the driving force in entertainment and journalism.

A handful of such corporations now control US media: Rupert Murdoch's News Corporation (FOX, HarperCollins, *New York Post, Weekly Standard, TV Guide,* DirecTV, Hulu, and 35 TV stations), General Electric (NBC, CNBC, MSNBC, Telemundo, Bravo, Universal Pictures, and 28 TV stations), Time Warner (AOL, CNN, Warner Bros., *People, Time,* and 130 other magazines), Disney (ABC, Disney Channel, ESPN, Pixar Animation Studios, and 10 TV and 72 radio stations), Viacom (Paramount Pictures, MTV, Comedy Central, Nickelodeon, and 183 US radio stations), and CBS (CBS Television, Showtime and 30 other cable channels, Random House, Simon and Schuster, and GameSpot).[29]

Profit making aside, let's not forget to mention why some people favor this consolidation. Increased efficiencies are often put forward in defending large-scale institutions through economies of scale and enhanced bargaining leverage. Huge operations can reduce expenses and even pass savings along to consumers. Companies with a global reach can sell their products around the world, decentralize their manufacturing operations, and capitalize on labor pools in nations where people work for less money. The main problem with the economies-of-scale argument, for all its apparent logic, is that the benefits of the enterprise are rarely shared equally. In almost all cases, the corporate profits accumulate in greater proportion among managers and shareholders than among low-level employees. Considering these dynamics on a global scale means that rich people and wealthy nations benefit at the expense of others.

Content Matters

Let's examine the narratives that movies, television, and other commercial media popularize. What kinds of stories are most likely to emerge in our new media economy? On one hand we find stories about human desire—for romance, adventure, or success. In other instances we see stories of human difference—about circumstances, actions, and thoughts that locate characters outside the banality of "normal" existence. Both types of stories—about desire and difference—exert a powerful influence on the popular imagination. And even though such narratives may entertain or even inspire many viewers, they can also alienate and degrade others. Replicated on a huge scale for audiences around the globe, the forces of desire and difference project a mind-set that separates viewers from those viewed. Consider how media generate a "cult of celebrity"—the relentless public fascination with famous personalities. A consideration of media history reveals how this phenomenon developed, starting with the introduction of movies. Because people across the country could for the first time enjoy the same movies, unlike with the traveling vaudeville acts that preceded them, this uniformity of experience created "national" celebrities. Fed by the novel form of newsreel publicity, movie audiences could vicariously "follow" stars as they traveled, got married, or did just about anything. America's first commercial radio station was launched in 1920. In less than a decade, the nation was obsessed with radio personalities, many of whom morphed into TV stars following World War II.

As with movies and radio, every new medium has generated its own array of bigger-than-life figures. The larger the medium has become, the more distant the personalities have seemed from the daily lives of audiences. Television theorist Clive James asserts that true fame was almost unknown until the end of the nineteenth century, simply due to the absence of global mass media.[30] According to James, the first genuine national celebrity of this kind was Charles Lindbergh, known first for his historic 1927 transatlantic air flight and later for the national upset over the kidnapping of his son. James distinguishes between fame (the phenomenon of being famous) and celebrity (fame heightened by media coverage). James argues that we have lost touch with merit-based fame contingent "on some kind of achievement."[31] Instead many people today are simply famous for being famous.

The earlier type of merit-based celebrity derived from success as an entertainer, journalist, athlete, author, or artist or from noteworthy work as an attorney, physician, or political leader. Then there are those famous for being born into families like the Barrymores, Hiltons, or Kennedys. But increasingly, media itself has become the driving force in creating fame. This new kind of fame has a novel quality, according to critic Bob Greene, because it no longer requires paying any dues. Greene believes that television has made the difference. Before TV people had to do something important or demonstrate some sort of talent. But since the ascendance of television, especially reality TV, Greene argues, the audiences have become the creators. Now someone can "become famous not for doing, but merely for being."[32] Often hyped by heavy media exposure, the cult of celebrity rivets our attention on the famous but also on otherwise unexceptional people who have wandered into the media spotlight. This sort of celebrity includes reality show contestants or wealthy characters like Kim Kardashian.

This world of celebrity matters because it has social effects. The distance from which they perceive celebrities renders audiences invisible and powerless, in effect silencing viewers who find themselves surrounded by media in their daily lives. Considering that these viewers "pay" for television programs with their time (often while enduring advertising pitches), it is striking that audiences remain so absent from the world presented by mass media. While occasionally making an appearance on laugh tracks or as a form of supporting cast for shows "filmed before a live studio audience," the viewing public is rarely seen. And when these audience members do get on screen, as in some variety programs or game shows, we see them as wildly enthusiastic crowds or as awkward individuals stammering before the unexpected gaze of the camera. This image of the hapless spectator has been extended in the cinema verité styling of long-form reality shows like *Survivor* and *Celebrity Apprentice,* but these shows are really close relatives of scripted dramas. Viewers of *Survivor* may assume they are watching the wilderness struggles of contestants in a genuine, real-time context, but in actuality, these programs are meticulously constructed narratives pieced together in the editing room. In popular scripted dramas like *NCIS* and *The Mentalist,* in which all the action is planned and even rehearsed before filming, it is not unusual for fifty to one hundred hours of material to be taped for a single episode. But in the unpredictable realm of reality TV, hours of raw footage can exceed two hundred per episode. And often even that much footage isn't enough to create a coherent narrative, at which point story lines are simply invented during the editing process using otherwise unrelated shots.

How do celebrities spend their days? Do they ever sit alone and watch TV? Are their lives anything like yours or mine? In one remarkable moment in the 2012 presidential campaign, FOX News broadcast a surreptitiously recorded segment of videotape showing President Barack Obama by himself on a park bench eating a hoagie. Commentators assailed Obama for degrading his office because he didn't look "presidential" when in fact he had simply been filmed doing something that regular people do. The wall between Obama's reality and his celebrity had been breached—and that provided an excuse for partisan outrage. The story shows how media spectacle alienates viewers from their actual lives, in this case suggesting that our everyday behavior is beneath the character of someone we respect and regard as a leader. The 1990s program *Lifestyles of the Rich and Famous* sent a similar message in documenting the enormous houses and extravagant lives of performers, athletes, and otherwise wealthy people. In the 2000s viewers were similarly taunted with images of wealth in the long-running program *Who Wants to Be a Millionaire?* broadcast in over forty nations through 2010. In recent years many cable systems have begun to feature WealthTV, a twenty-four-hour network specifically targeting the nation's "highest-income households."

Finally, content issues notwithstanding, it bears remembering that the formal structure of mass media reinforces any messages of disempowerment. Television operates in a one-directional form of address, except in rarely used interactive formats. People may receive its messages, but they cannot talk back. Movies have always had the same effect. Contrary to popular opinion, computers mostly do the same thing. Despite popular notions of the Internet as a two-directional "interactive" medium, online games generally offer only the illusion of true dialogue. Popular sites like GameSpot and Yahoo! Games may allow visitors to choose among and play games, but these choices are invariably limited by what the site makes available. The illusion of choice in online game play is but a microcosm of the pseudo-freedom offered in the larger commercial marketplace. Yet the sense of empowerment imparted by interactive media has made computer games the most rapidly expanding sector of today's entertainment industry.

Theme Parks and Disneyland

Much of this chapter has addressed the role of media and virtual environments in shaping our lives. We have considered what goes on inside our minds as we see and inhabit a world of images. But what about the "real" world? What happens when the images we see in movies or on TV take physical form as places? How do we imagine imaginary worlds as physical environments? In a way idealized images of the real world have always influenced architecture. Public buildings, places of worship, monuments, apartment buildings, and houses—all these to some extent reflect a desire to create a "world" to occupy.

Architecture surrounds us to such an extent that we often forget it is there. But like images or movies, architecture conveys meaning, expresses a point of view, and is never a neutral medium. Architecture literally sets the stage on which we play out the stories of our lives in the physical spaces we inhabit and visit. Architecture creates "worlds" that satisfy and convey human desires and needs and the politics that go with them. People think about architecture a little bit when picking out apartments, dorm rooms, or homes—figuring out how they will fill a space with their belongings. But most of the time, architecture remains in the background of our minds, as something we either take for granted or recognize that we can do little to change. The apparent permanence of built spaces allows us to forget about them as we concentrate on the things that do change in our lives. And we assume that the ways buildings and spaces are constructed are neutral, benign, and certainly safe. In fact, it is a function of government and law to insure that buildings are properly put together, with permitting agencies and inspectors to enforce standards. But while architecture sits in the background of our consciousness, it actually plays an enormous role in how we perceive reality, make choices, and even go about our daily lives.

Nowhere has the impulse to create imaginary spaces in our physical environment become more pronounced as in the rarified worlds of amusement and theme parks. Such places emerged from the confluence of several traditions, from common parks and architectural landmarks, to the more specialized genre of public gardens and fairs, to the exotic worlds of carnivals and expositions. The concept of idealized public spaces has a long history. Common public parks date to the 1500s, when nation-states began developing what we would now call government bureaucracies and the services they provide. At times the result of private philanthropy, pastoral preserves grew with urbanization and the perceived need to set aside land for common use and recreation. The United States established its national park system in 1864, when President Abraham Lincoln signed a bill that established the Yosemite Grant and its now famous federal grounds. Elsewhere in the world, wealthy families commonly set aside land to promote wildlife and hunting stock.

But in the nineteenth century the impulse to create fantasy environments assumed a more theatrical posture. Construction itself took on a grandiose dimension, with the completion of the Imperial Palace in Kyoto (1855), the Brooklyn Bridge in New York (1883), and the Eiffel Tower in Paris (1889). This trend toward more elaborate public displays of industrialization also appeared in fairs and so-called pleasure gardens—both precursors of what we now know as amusement parks. Beginning in the Elizabethan period, the fair evolved into a center for amusement—with food, games, and a variety of attractions. By the nineteenth century, England had also developed public gardens as a more elaborate manifestation of the urge to escape the urban world. In the United States, state and county fairs emerged to showcase agriculture and local culture, while in Germany Oktoberfest featured not only beer but also the new genre of amusement attractions.

With the launch of huge expositions and world's fairs in the mid-1800s—enabled by advances in transportation and technology—grand events, wondrous places, and "spectacles" began occurring. World's fairs originated in the French tradition of national exhibitions, a practice that culminated with the French Industrial Exposition of 1844 held in Paris. The opening of the Crystal Palace at the London World Exposition of 1851 offered opportunities for novel experience and armchair tourism with miniature villages, automated games, dioramic toys, and every imaginable "modern" carnival attraction. Similar events celebrating the era of industrialization took place in Sydney (1879), New Orleans (1884), Brussels (1887), Barcelona (1888), and dozens of other cities around the world.

On a more local level, fairs, circuses, and carnivals have always been with us as well. Running the gambit from the spectacular to the tawdry, periodic and impromptu festivities or traveling road shows have arisen in nearly every world culture. Russian philosopher Mikhail Bakhtin theorized the "carnivalesque" as a naturally developing form of public gathering that allowed people to blow off steam, subvert authority, or simply have fun.[33] In more basic terms, carnivals and circuses conveyed a protean form of popular culture, which also explains why they have fostered worry and suspicion throughout history. To Bakhtin, such places and events are attractive precisely because they provide a space outside the confines of normal life, where conventions and rules may be temporarily suspended, and the unexpected is possible.

But something special happened in the United States in the twentieth century. The introduction of electric trolley lines in the 1890s made beaches and leisure parks more accessible to working-class patrons, as electricity enabled the development of new kinds of amusements: penny arcades, shooting galleries, games of chance, and carousel rides. By the turn of the century, an enhanced kind of leisure park had opened, notably Brooklyn's Coney Island and the nation's first Kiddie Park in San Antonio, Texas. In the 1920s, Walter Knott, a farmer in California's Orange County, sold berries from a roadside stand that also included a restaurant selling fried chicken. To entertain waiting crowds, Knott introduced a ghost town in the 1940s and eventually began charging admission. Called Knott's Berry Farm, the amusement area today claims to be America's first theme park.

Yet a single individual stands out in the history of theme parks and remains an icon of popular culture. A true renaissance figure, Walt Disney was an artist, technological innovator, and visionary capitalist of the highest order. But in the context of this discussion, he deserves note for one particular idea. Perhaps more than anyone in world history, Disney succeeded in grafting media images onto the physical world. The characters in his movies became toys and other products in a way that had never happened before. And his imaginary landscapes became real places that people could visit and even inhabit.

After years of commercial success in the movie business, Walt Disney began to envision a physical space for his imaginary world. Original plans to launch a "Mickey Mouse Park" near Disney's Burbank, California, movie studio were rejected by city officials because they feared the idea of having a permanent carnival in town. So Disney found a plot of farmland in Orange County's Anaheim to build a park that opened in 1955. Some historians assert that Disney drew his inspiration from close-by Knott's Berry Farm. But Disney took the theme park idea to new heights.

Much has been written about the ideology and moral program implicit in Disneyland's vision of idealized childhood, cleanliness, and the control necessary to keep the Disney image intact. But in the context of this book, credit must be given to Disney for his vision of worlding, his recognition of the powerful impulse to experience a fantasy made real. Disney arrived at the perfect moment in history to deliver a postwar escapist fantasy world to a new suburban culture. Disneyland imprinted itself on the consciousness of the newly born baby boom generation and created a template for others to replicate, including Great America Parks, Legoland, Magic Mountain, Six Flags, Universal Studios Hollywood, and many others. Early theme parks differed from public parks in several ways, most notably in charging fees for attractions or admission to their grounds. Also, in the context of worlding, the new generation of privately developed theme parks recognized the need to reinforce their separation from public land. Theme park developers soon erected fences and barricades to make them hard to see from the outside, enhancing their aura as special places removed from the ordinary world.

As theme parks developed in the post–World War II era, roller coasters and thrill rides would become increasingly immersive, taking patrons into interior spaces and eventually into virtual reality simulators. All of this heightened the experience of "leaving" the real world for a journey into an imaginary space. As anyone who has experienced a theme park knows, this immersive experience can be quite powerful. The sensation of entering a fantasized visual world is reinforced by the physical experience of the moving ride. A number of factors come into play, often simultaneously. Most significant is the loss of control that riders experience. One's body is quite literally taken over by the gravitron, twister, or water flume—a sensation that yields both excitement and a measure of contained fear. Another factor is surprise, the experience of not knowing (at least initially) what is going to happen. Finally, modern theme park rides—like early roller coasters—add the key ingredient of perceived risk. All these elements combine to remove audiences briefly, yet powerfully, from their normal world experience and take them into another realm. In some ways experiencing theme park attractions can be equated with viewing an engaging adventure or horror movie—there's a transitory moment of exhilaration or fear that quickly disperses, returning the patron to the safety and comfort of the "real" world.

Notes

1. See Judith Halberstam, *In a Queer Time and Place: Transgender Bodies, Subcultural Lives* (New York: New York University Press, 2005).

2. Sherry Turkle, *Alone Together: Why We Expect More from Technology and Less from Each Other* (New York: Basic Books, 2011).

3. See Gilles Deleuze and Félix Guattari, *A Thousand Plateaus: Capitalism and Schizophrenia* (Minneapolis: University of Minnesota Press, 1987). In this work, the authors assert that conventional categories of economy and the mind inadequately describe human existence.

4. "Global Internet Users Cross 1-bn Mark in Dec," *Economic Times,* January 23, 2009, http://economictimes.indiatimes.com (accessed February 10, 2011).

5. *Making New Technologies Work for Development,* Human Development Report 2001, United Nations Development Programme, http://hdr.undp.org/en/reports/global/hdr2001 (accessed February 10, 2009).

6. Ibid., chs. 2, 10.

7. Ibid. See also, "English," in *Ethnologue: Languages of the World,* ed. M. Paul Lewis (Dallas, TX: SIL International, 2009), http://ethnologue.com (accessed October 18, 2012).

8. "Statistics on Texting," Articles Base, February 21, 2009, www.articlesbase.com/business-ideas-articles/statistics-on-texting-784182.html (accessed August 19, 2010).

9. All information about OnStar comes from Shanna Freeman, "How OnStar Works," How Stuff Works, http://auto.howstuffworks.com/onstar2.htm (accessed August 20, 2011).

10. "Kinect Confirmed as Fastest Selling Consumer Electronics Device in History," *Telegraph,* March 10, 2011, www.telegraph.co.uk/technology/

video-games/8371871/Kinect-sells-faster-than-iPhone-and-iPad.html (accessed January 13, 2012).

11. Howard Rheingold, *The Virtual Community: Homesteading on the Electronic Frontier* (Cambridge, MA: MIT Press, 2000).

12. James Cramer, *Getting Back to Even* (New York: Simon and Schuster, 2009).

13. Thomas L. Friedman, *The Lexus and the Olive Tree: Understanding Globalization* (New York: Farrar, Straus, and Giroux, 2000); *The World Is Flat 3.0: A Brief History of the Twenty-First Century* (New York: Picador, 2007); *Hot, Flat, and Crowded: Why We Need a Green Revolution and How It Can Renew America* (New York: Farrar, Straus, and Giroux, 2008); *That Used to Be Us: How America Fell behind in the World It Invented and How We Can Come Back* (New York: Farrar, Straus, and Giroux, 2011).

14. Thomas L. Friedman, excerpt from *The Lexus and the Olive Tree,* www.thomaslfriedman.com/lexusolivetree.htm (accessed December 16, 2011).

15. As cited in David Michael Smith, "The Growing Revolt against Globalization," Impactpress.com, www.impactpress.com/articles/augsep02/globalization8902.html (accessed December 18, 2011).

16. Smith, "The Growing Revolt against Globalization."

17. Aristotle, *The Basic Works of Aristotle,* ed. Richard McKeon (New York: Modern Library, 2001).

18. Marshall McLuhan and George B. Leonard, "The Future of Education: The Class of 1989," *Look Magazine,* February 21, 1967, 23–24.

19. Henry A. Giroux, *Popular Culture, Schooling and Everyday Life* (South Hadley, MA: Bergin and Garvey, 1989), ix.

20. Nigel Spivey, *How Art Made the World* (New York: Random House, 2005), 34.

21. John Belton, *American Cinema/American Culture* (New York: McGraw-Hill, 1994), 17.

22. Ella Shohat and Robert Stam, *Unthinking Eurocentrism: Multiculturalism and the Media* (New York: Routledge, 1994), 103.

23. Jan Pieterse, *White on Black: Images of Africa and Blacks in Western Popular Culture* (New Haven, CT: Yale University Press, 1992), 77.

24. Max Horkheimer and Theodore Adorno, *The Dialectic of Enlightenment,* trans. John Cumming (New York: Herder and Herder, 1972).

25. Bureau of Labor Statistics, *American Time Use Survey* (Washington, DC: US Department of Labor, 2011).

26. "Poverty Now Comes with a Color TV," *Christian Science Monitor,* 2005, http://articles.moneycentral.msn.com (accessed April 21, 2011).

27. Norman Herr, "Television and Health," California State University, Northridge, www.csun.edu/science/health/docs/tv&health.html (accessed April 21, 2011).

28. Newton Minow, "Vast Wasteland Speech," delivered to the National Association of Broadcasters, May 9, 1961, available at www.janda.org/b20/News%20articles/vastwastland.htm (accessed April 21, 2011).

29. "Ownership Chart: The Big Six," Free Press, www.freepress.net/ownership/chart/main (accessed January 5, 2012).

30. Clive James, *On Television* (New York: Picador, 1991).

31. Clive James, "Save Us from Celebrity," *The Independent,* October 28, 2005, www.independent.co.uk/news/media/clive-james-save-us-from-celebrity-512908.html (accessed April 27, 2011).

32. Bob Greene, "The New Stardom Doesn't Require Paying Any Dues," *Jewish World Review,* September 14, 2000, http://en.wikipedia.org/wiki/Celebrity (accessed April 27, 2011).

33. Mikhail Bakhtin, *Rabelais and His World* (Bloomington: Indiana University Press, 1941).

Chapter Five
Destination America

The American Dream exerts a powerful influence on the real and imaginary worldviews of many. The idea of the American Dream is rooted in the nation's founding documents, promising unbounded freedom to attain whatever one desires. What would happen if a real estate developer used the idea of the American Dream to build a shopping mall in a heavily multiethnic small town in the United States? What effect would the commercialization of all things American have on the local community? What would the constructed "American" world look like? One stunning example of this idea is found in California businessman Rick Caruso's recently opened Americana project. The Americana is a state-of-the-art "shopping and lifestyle" enterprise built on the rubble of a demolished section of downtown Glendale, California, a shining replica "world" of small-town America created by pushing out the real-world immigrant inhabitants of a California community so that the old Glendale downtown could become a quasi–tourist attraction.

The Americana is in some ways its own story, but in other ways it typifies what is now taking place across the United States and around the globe, as the "worlds" we traverse are increasingly commercialized and "scripted." With the Americana one finds the same style of world creation perfected by Walt Disney in the theme parks discussed in the previous chapter. In recent years, mall developers have shown how much they have learned from creators of fantasy environments in launching what are termed "themed malls."

Google the word "Americana," and you'll get a definition of US folk culture. Try "Caruso," and you'll find the biography of a famous tenor. Search for the two together, and you get the corporate website of one of America's most ruthless and aggressive land speculators—a West Coast developer that is making history in how it transforms neighborhoods and towns into commercial carnival shows. Caruso Affiliates specializes in creating what it terms "town centers," replica worlds of main streets and village squares in otherwise noncommercial zones. Recently unveiling the Americana in Glendale, however, Caruso has done something remarkable: despite heated local opposition, the company acquired 1 million square feet in the heart of downtown and refashioned four city blocks as a faux nineteenth-century town square—paving over any traces of the community that had been there.

In wiping out a major portion of historic Glendale, the Americana is an extraordinary example of the new migration of shopping malls from suburban to urban real estate. This shift has a number of implications, not the least of which is the obliteration of American small towns. It's part of the nation's ongoing transformation of public space into a private world. The wholesale takeover of American downtowns also signals a disturbing trend toward replacing local governance with corporate management. For these reasons, an examination of projects like the Americana can yield insights into the implications—both positive and negative—of the ongoing "malling of America."

From one perspective, a retail development like the Americana in Glendale might be seen as a healthy sign of adaptation to contemporary times and new business models. After all, the shopping mall is the essence of American retail, having emerged during the post–World War II suburban housing boom through the convergence of retailing and the automobile. The history of the shopping mall is a uniquely North American phenomenon whose genesis is often credited to Austrian-born architect Victor Gruen, who first recognized the opportunity presented by moving retailing away from the dense, commercial downtown to largely untapped markets in residential suburbs. Gruen's formula—contained spaces with stores attached, away from downtown, accessible only by car—would eventually become the preferred way to build retail spaces across the United States.

Key differences between downtown retail areas and shopping malls lie in their ownership and to whom they are answerable in terms of governance. Urban downtown commercial districts are sites of competing business interests and regulation by municipal governments. As a result the growth and governance of downtown areas at least nominally reflect the will of citizens and their elected officials. In contrast, large corporations or individual CEOs, who are answerable to shareholders and only indirectly to city regulators, run shopping malls. Advocates of such arrangements often cite the benefits of the business-management model in its ability to make quick decisions and to respond to customer needs free from bureaucratic red tape or long-term worries about the public aside from its purchasing preferences.

In most instances, malls and shopping centers pop up in undeveloped real estate on the outskirts of cities, where lower land prices have enabled construction of expansive suburban tracts. Frequently these new residential and commercial enterprises are attractive to developers because they lie outside the boundaries of municipal taxation and regulation. As Joel Garreau wrote in his classic *Edge City: Life on the New Frontier,* "We moved our homes out past the traditional idea of what constituted a city.... Then we wearied of returning downtown for the necessities of life, so we moved our marketplaces out to where we lived."[1] This is exactly the dynamic that suburban expansion has been creating throughout the United States, and nowhere is it more pronounced than in the rapidly growing suburban landscape of Southern California, where the phenomenon of suburban sprawl was first recognized.

But what happens to the original cities that suburbanites leave behind? What occurs when residents who can afford the price move to the suburbs and businesses follow them? What takes place when entire parts of the country begin to depopulate as people move to the sunny regions where suburbia is booming? One simply needs to examine the aging metropolises of the Northeast and the Midwestern rust belt cities. As money moves to the periphery, metropolitan centers start to deteriorate—leaving behind those who can't afford to leave. Urban land loses value, city budgets shrink, and services decline in a downward spiral that feeds on itself. Poverty and crime increase in blighted neighborhoods, where the police force becomes the most visible sign of what was once a functioning city government. When this process first emerged in the 1960s and 1970s, angry urban populations that found themselves locked into city ghettos responded with riots, burning the rotted remains of many cities to the ground. This prompted the federal government to step in, first with troops and later with money for federal housing projects and urban reconstruction projects. Eventually, in the 1980s and 1990s, cities that could muster the resources began efforts to reconceptualize downtown areas, especially those that could claim some kind of "historic" dimension like Baltimore, Boston, Chicago, and Philadelphia. The process was not always a smooth one, as urban minority residents often found themselves pushed and squeezed out of affordable housing in a process James Baldwin termed "negro removal." The slow return of residents to refurbished slums and urban industrial districts continues today in a process known as "gentrification."

In most large cities the job of urban renewal was and remains too large a task for even the largest corporations. Federal, state, and local governments have done the job—occasionally in collaboration with business interests—motivated by the long-term financial benefits of reduced poverty and crime, as well as the promise of future tax revenues. And to a large extent, such government investments in downtown renewal have indeed paid off very well. This redevelopment success raises an intriguing possibility. What if a city were small enough and sufficiently run down for a huge corporation to assume the job of downtown redevelopment by itself? The idea wouldn't be that radical. In recent years, corporations have assumed the role formerly occupied by government in the operation of schools, hospitals, prisons, and even some of the nation's military operations in Iraq. In some cities, organized retail centers or factory outlets have been part of the calculus of an overall city plan—as in Atlanta, Houston, Manhattan, Milwaukee, Rochester, and San Francisco. And town-center malls are nothing particularly new, with retail developments of all sorts fashioning themselves to imitate the form of a forgotten America. But Caruso's dismantling and repackaging of an actually existing city center is a stunning innovation.

Americana Dreams

From a developer's perspective, the Americana is a true wonder of contemporary urban renewal. Like other Caruso malls, it is meant to evoke another world not unlike the famous Main Street in Disneyland. The choice of the name Americana seems strategic, given the racial and ethnic character of its location and the diversity of its shoppers, the majority of whom are recent immigrants to the United States. It's like a retail version of Ellis Island, but dressed up for the landed aristocracy. With its sumptuous décor and expensive flourishes, Caruso's new enterprise beckons its patrons with the visible trapping of the American Dream: lingerie from Kelly Hicks, handbags from Vera Bradley, and diamonds from Tiffany. Atop the Americana's retail properties are 238 apartments renting for between $2,000 and $5,000 monthly and 1,000 condominiums costing $700,000 to $2 million. Among the tenants' unique "lifestyle" amenities is room service offering a complete menu twenty-four hours per day. As with many theme malls, the Americana is set in a particular time and place, specifically, the turn-of-the-century United States, and features the modernist industrial imagery of the era. Massive, exposed steel girders support the elevator inside the shopping area. Faux-brick store exteriors with decorative scrollwork and other baroque architectural touches offset these details.

In the Americana's main square lies a huge green lawn, itself no small feat in the desert climate of Glendale. Rising from its center, a tremendous computer-controlled fountain flows around a bronze statue of a flying male figure gilded in twenty-three-karat gold. The eighteen-foot statue, titled *Spirit of American Youth,* replicates a monument at France's Omaha Beach Memorial. (Nearly every Caruso project features statuary of children playing in water.) Stepping from your car into the nine-story parking structure, you enter what appears to be the spacious lobby of the Ritz-Carlton, complete with glittering chandelier, ornate elevator, and front desk staffed by uniformed attendants. The effect is so convincing that many visitors to the Americana have mistaken the parking garage for a functioning luxury resort. "People keep coming up and asking about room rates," a pertly blazered attendant explained to me during a recent visit, "but we are the concierge service." The presence of uniformed help is very much a part of the Americana's world. At valet parking one encounters a row of perhaps a dozen parking attendants in imperial white military dress. By the elevators is a character attired like Sergeant Pepper. Inside the Americana, helpers in blue hotel uniforms are everywhere. Even the security guards look like bellhops. The effect is transformative. Shopping at the Americana is like taking a vacation one can't really afford. At least, that was the response of many people who visited the mall in its opening weeks. Many shoppers I spoke with said the goods were too pricy for them to purchase, but walking around and looking at the place was quite an experience. This is where shopping mall commerce and theme park entertainment come together, both in the adulation of a single value: wealth.

It should come as no surprise that not everyone has been thrilled by the Americana. Opposition to the mall goes back more than a decade. Originally, the project was criticized by many Glendale citizens and business owners, who feared it would put a strain on city services, bankrupt existing stores, and exacerbate congestion in a city already trying to cope with a recent 50 percent population increase. As one Glendale citizen wrote to the *LA Times,* "Caruso's naming of his development project is an affront to the name 'America.' It is as conceptually removed by distance as it is by philosophy. It is a project conceptualized of an Italian/European motif made possible by the use of dual coercions: The taking of private property by the threat of government action (eminent domain), and the taking of taxpayers' money for a commercial venture."[2] But with shrewd legal maneuvers and the financial backing of a new majority in the city council, Caruso was able to get his way as he has done in other municipalities that tried to stop him. A man not known for a sense of irony, Caruso asserted that opposition to the Americana was "un-American" because it threatened free market competition.

Beyond local economics lie deeper concerns about the implications of surrendering the center of a city's public space to private interests. For one thing, it means that the growth of the area and access to it are no longer defined by Glendale itself. Like Disneyland, the Americana is a highly regulated world that excludes such annoyances as skateboarders, vagrants, large dogs, and anything that might alter its dreamlike ambiance. A former Los Angeles police commissioner, Caruso has publicly lamented the "crime and dirt" of downtown Los Angeles. In short, the Americana is a place to get away from urban problems rather than be reminded of them or think about changing them.

On a deeper level, the Americana creates an environment in a former public space that is now completely defined by a specific kind of retail experience, what Caruso refers to as "the luxurious." The surrounding community—comprised heavily of working-class residents from Armenia, Iran, Latin America, and the Philippines—finds in the Americana a netherworld European aristocracy, with details emulating France, Italy, and, of course, the folklorist world of "Americana" décor. Shoppers find themselves surrounded by expensive-looking mall details like gold-plated statuary and imported trolley cars and by stores like Armani, Aveda, Calvin Klein, Lacoste, and Tiffany. Paying for the expensive goods on offer is the price of admission—along with parking available only in Americana lots. At the Americana, one can be wealthy and apart from one's daily existence. This is hardly an innocent phenomenon. Inherent in the public's experience of public spaces like the Americana is an articulation of deeper power relations. As Norman Klein explains,

> We must take each step on its own, and see the problem as ideological (program); epistemological (script); and ontological (reception). In other words, at the level of program, the political use of ideology is fundamental and must be studied that way (how political interest is manifested within codes generated to protect those at the top, or condemn their perceived enemies). At the level of script, there is a code of how knowledge is supposed to be set up, how the branches and winding paths reveal knowledge. And on the level of reception,

the virtual is always relative; there is always a crisis about real/unreal, a suture between the two that makes the story exciting.[3]

The Jewel City

The jury is still out regarding the long-term effect the Americana will have on the city of Glendale, although some observers have expressed apprehension. Despite some initial turnover among retail tenants, the Americana seems to have become something of a destination for casual dining and moviegoing, if not shopping. It's still not clear whether the Americana draws shopping dollars away from nearby businesses or gives Glendale a boost by luring added customers to the downtown. In either case, a lot of shopping can take place in Glendale, and the Americana's tax revenues benefit the community.

Often called "the Jewel City," Glendale has been characterized as a "typical" American small town. Located just miles from the heart of downtown Los Angeles, Glendale is one of eighty-eight Los Angeles County municipalities, like Compton, Inglewood, Long Beach, Pasadena, Pomona, Redondo Beach, Santa Monica, and Torrance. Incorporated as a city in 1906, Glendale was a sleepy, small town in its early decades, known as the birthplace of the Baskin-Robbins and Bob's Big Boy chains, as well as the West Coast headquarters during the 1960s of the American Nazi Party. With a current population of two hundred thousand, Glendale has a modest downtown, a large expanse of suburban neighborhoods, and several large employers known for their family-friendly fare: DreamWorks, Neopets, Nestlé, and International House of Pancakes. Glendale's biggest attraction for tourists is the Forest Lawn Cemetery, famous as the final resting place of celebrities including Gene Autry, Bette Davis, Lucille Ball, Buster Keaton, Liberace, Ricky Nelson, John Ritter, and Rod Steiger.

Glendale's population doubled in the post–World War II era and has continued to swell in recent years with a large influx of immigrants from Armenia, Iran, Latin America, and the Philippines. Today the majority of Glendale's population consists of foreign-born residents, giving it the vitality of American "melting-pot" diversity. In Glendale government, the surge of immigrant groups has transformed a former bastion of Anglo-Saxon, Protestant political power into an Armenian stronghold. Accounting for 40 percent of the city's population, the Armenian presence in Glendale has worried other residents who complain about the outdoor grilling of Armenian restaurants and resent the city's lowering of

American flags on the annual Armenian Genocide Commemoration Day. Fights and rivalries in Glendale high schools have been a source of rising concern—and of consternation for businesspeople like Rick Caruso who want Glendale to be perceived as a safe place for shopping and leisure.

Given its character as cultural melting pot, Glendale might seem a logical site for a project named "Americana." From this perspective, the interior character of Caruso malls might seem to mirror—at least partially—the diverse California communities in which they have been popping up. Caruso is fond of appointing his projects with an international assortment of decorative details—including metal kiosks imported from Luxembourg and an eighteenth-century chandelier from Czechoslovakia with 1,220 sparkling crystals—reminiscent of European promenades and plazas, where "style makes a grand entrance."[4] The Caruso corporate website describes the corporation's vision to fashion "quality destinations that focus on people places such as parks and fountains integrated with upscale retail. Reading the mood of today's savvy consumer, the company employs the richest materials and design integrity to create meticulously detailed environments that feel inviting, safe and comfortable."[5]

Just how well the vision of Caruso style fits with Glendale and its surrounding areas is unclear. The average annual household income in Glendale of $41,000 is about same as that throughout the United States. With a typical family size of 3.3 people, this works out to a monthly income of $1,000 per person. As in most of Los Angeles County, rents in Glendale take a bigger chunk of people's income than elsewhere, with one-bedroom apartments averaging $1,660 per month. This means Glendale residents are more pinched than most people in paying for food, clothing, college tuition—or shopping for extras at a mall. This is especially the case at Caruso malls. At Caruso's Grove complex adjacent to LA's Fairfax District Farmers Market, a typical shopper's excursion amounts to an expenditure of $126. Such spending hardly fits the budget of most Glendale families. Nor does the price tag on the Americana's housing units, where condominium rents start at $2,000 and run as high as $5,000 monthly. Clearly the Americana is trolling for bigger fish. Or is it?

Casino Capitalist

To many people, forty-eight-year-old Rick Caruso is a model of citizenship and enlightened business leadership. His company, Caruso Affiliated, has emerged as the largest retail-development corporation in America, investing over $1 billion in projects generating $80 million in tax revenues and creating nineteen thousand jobs. Caruso malls have been successful, typically doing 75 percent more business than the national average. On the model of casino capitalist Donald Trump, Caruso is the public face of the enterprise, and he very much looks the part.[6] Clean-cut and athletic in $6,000 Brioni suits, Caruso enjoys a lively game of tennis and a glass of Chivas scotch. He looks a bit like a young Tony Franciosa with a suntan. Caruso is a quintessential family man and father of four whose admirers speak of his "sweet, human quality." Born into affluence, the wealthy Republican grew up in Beverly Hills. Caruso became a real estate developer at twenty-six by buying land next to the LA airport and leasing it to car rental agencies like Dollar, founded by his father.[7] Despite working twelve-hour days, after an hour in the gym Caruso drives his four children to school every morning in a Bentley. He enjoys entertaining guests like Warren Christopher, Antonin Scalia, and neighbor Arnold Schwarzenegger at his ten-thousand-square-foot Brentwood home. Active in Los Angeles politics since his mid-twenties, Caruso was the 2008 financial cochair of the Mitt Romney presidential campaign. He served on the Los Angeles Police Commission, where he oversaw the controversial firing of African American LA police chief Gordon Parks. In this action, some of Caruso's temper emerged as he reportedly referred to a prominent city council member as "a bitch."

Get between Caruso and his business, and you really see his tough side. This has happened whenever a community has tried to block any of his sixteen mall projects, such as his waterfront project in San Francisco's East Bay, the Grove "lifestyle mall" in Los Angeles, and, most notably, the Americana. Launching the new mall was no simple task. The project was fought tooth and nail by an unlikely alliance of Glendale community groups and a rival mall development company. With their local economy sagging, merchants along Glendale's main commercial thoroughfare, Brand Avenue, worried about new competition. Big-box retailers like Tower Records and the Good Guys had already closed their branches, adding two more empty storefronts to the city's downtown. But business remained strong at the existing Glendale downtown mall, the Glendale Galleria, owned by Chicago-based development company General Growth. The drawing power of the Glendale Galleria made it the second-largest shopping mall in Los Angeles County. With 220 businesses, including department stores like Macy's and Nordstrom, discount merchants like JC Penney, Mervyns, and Target, and boutique retailers like Apple, Coach, Eddie Bauer, Godiva, Nine

West, Oakley, Steve Madden, and Talbot's, the Glendale Galleria catered to a wide economic spectrum, drawing from both the local community and the region at large. Although the Galleria easily accommodated its thousands of daily shoppers, Glendale's downtown often found itself choked with traffic from the mall. This made residents leery of yet another high-volume retail center.

Local opposition reached a breaking point in 2001, when it became public that the city was planning to contribute $77 million to the Caruso project in infrastructure improvements and administrative expenses—adding still more in additional police costs—and to lease the fifteen-acre downtown site to Caruso for a century at $1 per year. For its part, General Growth announced a $30-million alternative project to the Americana, while launching a protest against the proposed zoning changes the city was poised to make for Caruso. When it came time to make the decision, the Glendale City Council voted against the Americana. The city already had one of the largest downtown malls in California and didn't need more traffic and congestion. But the small town was no match for the mastermind developer.

Initially Caruso responded by angrily and publicly scuttling his plans. "To spend five years and $5 million to design a project and have a procedural issue stop us ... is beyond my comprehension," he said to the council.[8] "You think there is a better deal out there? Any developer worth its salt won't go anywhere near this place."[9] But Caruso wasn't finished. Also a skilled attorney, he sued General Growth while simultaneously backing the candidacies of enough city council members to give him a three-to-two majority. Caruso won the case against General Growth, netting $89 million in the judgment, and his city council friends reversed the council's previous decision. Caruso's success with Glendale municipal officials was so dramatic that the once-oppositional city council renamed a downtown street Caruso Avenue in his honor. The $324-million Americana broke ground in 2005 at a ceremony with Caruso himself pushing down a TNT detonator that demolished a structure on the site. An army of twenty-five hundred construction workers then converged on the place.

Be a Tourist in Your Own Town

As the construction dust settled in the months following the opening of the Americana, much of the initial public anxiety faded, as Glendale adapted to its new downtown "center" for better or for worse. Like most malls, the Americana does the lion's share of its business on weekends and during the evenings, when workday traffic has subsided. It's even possible that skyrocketing gasoline prices may have slightly lowered the number of cars on the road. Meanwhile, Rick Caruso moved on to new projects, like the one near Santa Barbara, where Monticello residents fought in vain against his takeover of a historic hotel as part of yet another scheme to convert a locality into the site of a town-center mall. For Caruso, it's simply back to business as usual in the "malling of America," a process that continues to take place across the country and a form of retail development that one rarely sees in other nations.

There is little doubt that large-scale malling is changing America. Today Americans spend a full quarter of their disposable income at the nation's 90,786 shopping malls, approximately $7,528 per person, or ten times the amount spent on Internet shopping.[10] This works out to $2.25 trillion, an amount equal to the gross domestic product of Germany. And those shopping centers take up a lot of space: nearly 7 billion square feet, or 245 square miles—four times the size of the District of Columbia. Malls also constitute one of the country's largest employment sectors, accounting for 12.6 million jobs, or 9 percent of the nonfarm workforce.

These statistics indicate the extent to which shopping malls both reflect and shape public retail preferences, as well as the underlying social attitudes behind them. In the media-saturated era of the early 2000s, contemporary society has increasingly become defined through visual information. Much entertainment, advertising, and news is delivered via electronic or print media that communicate more through images than text or speech. Media producers battle each other for the most compelling kinds of images, often typified by the idealized depictions of famous personalities. Through the artifice of television, film, and photography, people on the screen are made up, dressed, and enhanced digitally to look more perfect or glamorous than people in real life. By comparison the average person looks inadequate or defective. These perceptions are hardly lost on the beauty and clothing industries, which introduce endless products to improve people's complexions, shrink their waistlines, or make them look rich. Such imagery is so ubiquitous that viewers hardly notice the constant barrage. The ideal of flawless appearance seems as natural as sunshine.

The underlying message of our image-saturated world is that people need to emulate the idealized characters they see on the screen—a standard most people are never able to meet. Media representations of women depict waifish models, with perfect skin, flawless hair, and inexplicably large bust lines—all of this is genetically impossible for 99 percent of the population to achieve, even with the help of makeup or cosmetic surgery. Nevertheless, many people come to believe that how they look defines who they are. Newsstands overflow with magazines like *Allure, Cosmopolitan, Elle, Glamour, Mademoiselle,* and *Vogue,* which promote the same message of personal identity—and, by extension, individual value—defined by appearance.

If appearance and products define identity, retail sites rely similarly on images. Customers are drawn to stores that look reputable and attractive, shopping worlds that appear accessible and safe. When shopping malls first gained prominence in the 1960s and 1970s, they appealed to shoppers with efficiency, cleanliness, and contemporary styling. But as their numbers multiplied in the 1980s and 1990s, malls became difficult to distinguish from one another and often were ridiculed for the same cookie-cutter conformity as suburban housing developments. This is when specialty malls began to emerge, defined by historic periods, ethnic motifs, or specialty boutiques. Emerging from this mix in the early 2000s has been the "lifestyle center." Lifestyle centers occupy the opposite end of the commercial development spectrum from the outlet mall, which typically caters to a wider income range with bargain prices. The growth of lifestyle centers has occurred at the expense of traditional shopping malls, which require large sites of over 70 acres at a time when land prices are escalating. Lifestyle centers take up less land and generate higher revenues, often yielding close to $500 per square foot, compared to an average of $330 per square foot for a traditional mall.

The idealized town-center concept mall has emerged in the 2000s as a natural extension of mall worlding aesthetics, casting a nostalgic patina on standard mall ideals of safety and cleanliness. The quintessential replica small-town America is the famous Main Street in Disneyland. As Walt Disney himself described it, "Main Street, U.S.A. is America at the turn of the century—the crossroads of an era. The gas lamps and the electric lamps, the horse-drawn car and the auto car. Main Street is everyone's home town ... the heartland of America." Disney was well known in California as both an entertainment mogul and an ideologue. Disneyland and Disney products did more than simply cash in on the population bubble of baby boomer offspring. Beneath his outward appearance as a friendly patriarch and creator of children's fare, Disney was a savage anti-Communist and a conservative political power broker. Disneyland was more than "the happiest place on earth." It was a repudiation of the urban landscape of mid-century Los Angeles, where poverty, pollution, traffic, crime, and nonwhite populations were all on the rise. Disney had taken his daughters to LA's Griffith Park carousel during World War II and "found it grimy and uncontrolled."[11] He deplored the disorder of crowds spilling out all over the place, as in Coney Island and older amusement parks, which Disney likened to bad neighborhoods. A protected enclave was the answer—a walled-off and guarded space where a utopian small town could be "imagineered" and maintained. As Norman Solomon explains, "Disneyland was to be cleaned continuously, like one of those new self-cleaning ovens, and would offer absolute immunity to the visitors, a sanctuary."[12]

Fast-forward a few decades to the present, and Los Angeles hasn't changed much. The air pollution has gone down, but the city's urban problems and the endless influx of humanity haven't stopped. With a population of 13 million, the Los Angeles metropolitan area spans 470 square miles, making it one of the most diverse counties in the United States—a municipality the size of a small country, where 224 languages are spoken. Walt Disney is long gone, but his legacy lives on in the media conglomerate that bears his name. The Disney Corporation operates Disneyland, Disneyworld, Walt Disney Imagineering, ABC Television, ESPN, Touchstone Pictures, Miramax Films, Hyperion Books, Hollywood Records, Radio Disney, the Soap Network, Family.com, Movies.com, and numerous other brands. The Disney name also is commemorated in the home of the Los Angeles Philharmonic, the downtown Disney Concert Hall designed by Frank Gehry. Beyond Southern California, Disney has recreated its Main Street in Orlando, Hong Kong, Paris, and the 355 Disney Stores worldwide.

The construction of the Americana in downtown Glendale extends the Disney "Main Street" worldview in physical terms. Glendale was the location of the very first Disney Store, which opened in 1987, and is visible from Disney corporate headquarters a few miles away in Burbank. Rick Caruso makes no secret of his admiration of Walt Disney and his philosophies, and he often quotes the legendary imagineer in articulating his objectives. Caruso publicly lamented the "dirt and crime" of downtown Los Angeles during his years on the LA Department of Water and Power and during his presidency of the LA Police Commission. Many in LA power circles believe Caruso, like Disney, would be an ideal candidate for the city's mayoralty. But like Disney, Caruso has deferred such an ambition, stating that public office would be too constraining for his maverick personality. Disney put it quite succinctly when he once quipped, "Why would I want to be a mayor when I am already a king?"[13]

To extend the metaphor, the Americana resembles nothing so much as a king's castle—it's a world unto itself. With its stores designed to face inward, the structure's exterior is composed of windowless fifty-foot walls painted to look like storefronts. The mall has one ground-level pedestrian entrance, facing a now empty Tower Records. To reach the street from the Americana's parking garage, patrons must traverse the entire mall. This isn't a design that any urban planner would recommend for building a downtown. The Americana is more like a fortress for keeping the rest of the world—and its problems—at a safe distance. Inside the Americana, one experiences an idealized vision of what a small town might be like if paint didn't age, dirt didn't exist, and no one were poor. The Americana is a bit like a children's storybook, or what Norman Klein calls a "scripted space."[14] Increasingly, environments like malls, casinos, and amusement parks are scripted to provide visitors a fantasy experience. Moving through the scripted space, people feel as though they are freely deciding where to go and what to see. But actually, they are navigating an immersive environment in which every option has already been predetermined—not unlike in a computer game.

The effects of the scripted space range from the obvious to the subtle. At the Americana attention is drawn to glittering statues and spectacular fountains in an atmosphere cleansed of urban noise and traffic. Visitors see no trash, or peeling paint, or homeless panhandlers. Most get their last glimpses of the world outside the mall as they are parking their cars. Inside, costumed security guards are everywhere, unlike on the streets of Glendale and greater Los Angeles where one rarely ever sees a police officer. The scripted atmosphere of the Americana is especially festive, animated with jazz bands, clown acts, free yoga lessons, storybooks read to kids, and even special "Monday Mommy Movies" especially intended for parents with wailing babies. For the most part, it seems like the mall's storybook narrative has taken the day. Articles in local newspapers about the Americana's opening were nearly all celebratory. The mall already has become a regular part of the city. Ultimately this is the effect of urban developments and their ideologies. Their causes and deeper meanings become accepted, naturalized, and ultimately forgotten. Meanwhile business at the Americana goes on as usual.

Notes

1. Joel Garreau, *Edge City: Life on the New Frontier* (New York: Anchor, 1992), 4.

2. Herbert Molano, "The New Medici vs. Capitalism, or Denouncing General Growth Is Anti-American," *Los Angeles Times,* January 16, 2005.

3. Norman M. Klein, *The Vatican to Vegas: A History of Special Effects* (New York: New Press, 2004), 328.

4. The Americana at Brand, www.americanaatbrand.com (accessed March 28, 2011).

5. "Development," www.carusoaffiliated.com (accessed May 28, 2010).

6. Susan Strange, *Casino Capitalism* (Manchester: Manchester University Press, 1997).

7. J'Amy Brown, "Ty Selling Miramar to Caruso?," *Santa Barbara Independent,* January 22, 2008, www.independent.com/news/2007/jan/22/ty-selling-miramar-to-caruso (accessed May 20, 2011).

8. Naush Bogossian, "Caruso Gives Up on Mall," The Free Library, www.thefreelibrary.com/CARUSO+GIVES+UP+ON+MALL.-a0114835070 (accessed May 20, 2010).

9. Ibid.

10. Dees Stribling, "Onward and Upward," *Shopping Centers Today,* October 2007, www.icsc.org/srch/sct/sct1007/onward_upward.php (accessed November 22, 2011).

11. Walt Disney, quoted in Klein, *The Vatican to Vegas,* 313.

12. Klein, *The Vatican to Vegas,* 316.

13. Walt Disney quoted in ibid., 202.

14. Klein, *The Vatican to Vegas,* 325.

CHAPTER SIX
VIRTUAL CULTURE

Virtual Worlds in Historical Perspective

Stories have always created virtual worlds in the minds of audiences. After all, the process of narrative that Aristotle described was really a mental process of following a story in one's mind and imagining what might happen next. But this "worlding" phenomenon took a dramatic leap with refinements in realistic rendering. The real wonder of Renaissance perspective painting and its infatuation with fine detail lay in the way it drew viewers into the picture. The images captured viewers' attention by obliging them to examine the detail. The illusion of depth helped viewers imagine that they were actually entering the pictorial space.

Throughout history people have traveled into imaginary visual worlds. Evolutionary psychologists have examined the human fascination with detailed images that afford viewers a perception of depth in space. Stephen and Rachel Kaplan have found that people are drawn instinctively to landscapes since such images create a sense of entry into the pictorial space.[1] The Kaplans also noticed a shared fondness among viewers for certain types of landscapes that give additional spatial clues that seem to invite exploration. The most engaging landscapes tend to center attention on a trail, roadway, or body of water connecting foreground and background. The presence of either a focal point or a distant view of the horizon enhances the visual integrity of the landscape, which further increases its appeal. Viewers are intrigued by this implied journey into the picture space due to the suggestion that they might learn something by immersing themselves further into the scene.[2]

Taking an anthropological approach to this phenomenon, Jay Appleton believes that hardwired instincts for safety drive our interest in pictures with deep-space perspective. Appleton has theorized what he terms a "prospect-and-refuge" inclination common to the human species.[3] We naturally seek a prospect, or safe vantage point, from which to survey a landscape and check for potential danger. In this process we also scan for a refuge in the form of an elevation or enclosure. Appleton says that these human preferences might explain why castles and houses on hillsides appear so frequently throughout the history of painting.[4]

While photography made pictures seem decidedly more "real" than ever before, efforts to make viewing even more immersive continued with experiments in 3-D techniques. Fascination with the photographic image fit perfectly with the new scientific ethos of the 1800s, driving all manner of experiments with lenses, viewing contraptions, and chemical processes. Keep in mind that depth perception comes from the bicameral vision created by a pair of eyes. The Renaissance one-point perspective and its later mechanization via photography brought imaging a long way, but the approximation of actual human sight was still elusive. Charles Wheatstone created the first stereographic images in 1838 by using two cameras, about an inch apart, to photograph a scene. Stereographic images were paired on cards that, held at the right distance from the eyes, provided a novel sense of pictorial depth.

But it wasn't simply the doubled imagery that made the stereograph successful. For anyone other than the most experienced viewer, the illusion of three-dimensionality would never readily occur without a handheld device to focus the eyes on two images simultaneously. The key to making this work came from the way the stereo viewing device blocked out everything else in one's field of vision. This combination of images and device created the illusion of leaving one world behind and entering another.

Cinematic experience is naturally adaptable to 3-D because this elimination of viewing distractions always occurs in a darkened theater. 3-D movies have cycled in and out of vogue with at least five iterations since they were first introduced in the 1920s. With each 3-D boom, audiences have had to wear special glasses, but most have done so willingly. Recent 3-D systems benefit further from technological advances yielding greater detail and larger projection sizes. The first IMAX theaters opened in the 1980s, showing movies shot on film stock almost double the size of the 35-mm industry standard. High-definition (HD) digital filmmaking technologies of the 2000s raised the bar even higher in terms of resolution and clarity, while further accentuating the illusion of depth with special effects. Nevertheless, digital 3-D still called for special glasses, not to mention specially designed movie projectors. The popularity of 3-D movies in the 2000s had one further effect. Prior to the advent of digital filmmaking, 3-D movies required specially adapted cameras. But when 3-D technology became computerized, it became possible to remaster older films. *Star Wars* (1977), *Titanic* (1997), *The Lion King* (1994), *Toy Story* (1995), *Monsters, Inc.* (2001), and *Beauty and the Beast* (1991) are just a few classic titles recently rendered in 3-D.

"Immersion" is the most recent term for movies' capacity to pull viewers into a virtual world. However, film scholars have for a long time discussed the uncanny ability of movies to help audiences "suspend disbelief" or enter the "diegetic space" and hence forget the world outside the picture frame. In the 1970s film theorist Christian Metz proposed two ways of describing this experience.[5] On one hand, in the isolation of a darkened movie theater, viewers imagine themselves inside the story being told, sometimes even as one of the characters in the unfolding story. On the other hand, viewers also sometimes unconsciously identify with the omniscient perspective of the camera, which suggests a masterful overview of the story. In both instances—whether viewers identify as characters in the narrative or as external onlookers—the mental process nearly always demands a temporary acceptance of the terms of the story.

Of course, stories have always worked this way. One has to let go of the outside world—at least for a little while—to keep up with the plot of any book or sitcom. Yet the implications of this process go a bit deeper. As the study and analysis of the movie-viewing process began to unfold, suspicions began to grow that this detachment from external realities could lead people astray. In some instances, psychologists also suggested that movies encouraged audiences to regress to states of childlike vulnerability, infantilizing them with a media technology capable of defining the world for them.

Before long, feminists and others noticed that particular stories seemed to get repeated in movies and other entertainment: men always seemed in control, women were ignored or treated as sex objects, and minorities were often mocked or villainized. Add to this that the entertainment industry of the 1970s and 1980s was mostly run by white heterosexual men who oversaw the studios, selected the films, authored the scripts, ran the cameras, and then sold the productions, and a certain kind of conspiracy seemed to emerge. Was it possible that the whole business was driven by the interests of predominately white, straight men?

This was the genesis of the term "male gaze" in film studies. But it doesn't take an academic degree to grasp this theory. Almost any movie or TV show can be used to test the idea of gendered cinematic point of view. In a well-known essay published in 1973, British feminist Laura Mulvey noted how movies usually arrange female characters within the frame to be viewed in certain ways.[6] More often than men, women are filmed facing the camera, and their appearance seems to be accented. As scenes unfold, women tend to be looked at by men. These formal conventions in the act of filming are then usually, although not always, reinforced by the story itself. The point is that most people never consciously recognize how much the camera is influencing them.

Are viewers really so naive about what they are seeing? This issue has raised its own controversy. Is it possible that audiences really regress into passive acceptance of what they experience in TV shows or movies? Do we always agree with the camera's implicit ideology? Here again, one can't really take issue with the premise that audiences must yield somewhat to the story for it to operate in their minds. But viewers are hardly so impressionable—certainly not viewers who since childhood have watched thousands of TV commercials that they know seek to manipulate them.

Media viewing is a complicated process. Audiences "read" TV and movies through an intellectual process much like that of reading a book. This act of interpreting written or visual media has been termed "coding." The linguist Ferdinand de Saussure described this coding as a systematic process of assigning symbols to thoughts.[7] Through such symbols as words or pictures, ideas are "encoded" by those sending the messages and later "decoded" by recipients. Notably, the process can't ensure that the message received will be the same as the one sent. People are constantly misunderstood or ignored when they exaggerate, as we see with advertising pitches.

The "reading" of cinematic or virtual worlds also can be seen as a kind of contest. While watching a movie, people exercise several mental processes, sometimes agreeing with the story and its premises, but at other times arguing with it in their minds, imagining different outcomes, and even rejecting it. It took a while for this idea of a mental "dialogue" in media viewing to be accepted. But things changed about two decades ago as educators and others began to examine the variety of ways ordinary people seemed to enjoy what they watched. With so many millions of people glued to TV sets and going to the movies, were they all being manipulated? Perhaps it was no coincidence that the entertainment industry itself began providing some of the answers through shows that assumed audiences could be critical viewers. Launched in 1975, *Saturday Night Live* (*SNL*) became an instant hit with its satiric skits that mimicked TV commercials and news programs. Highlighting the artificiality of television was inherently funny. Then as now, the *SNL* format centered on celebrity hosts for each episode, with these hosts often featured in comic versions of their own movies or TV shows.

The success of *SNL* comes from its appeal to media-savvy audiences capable of recognizing its satire as a critique of media artifice—and of authority more generally. *SNL* can turn its gun on posturing politicians and pompous newscasters or on such issues as racial stereotyping and homophobia in mass culture. The *SNL* genre would later be adapted by entertainers like Stephen Colbert and Jon Stewart, both of whom base their satire on a critique of big media. More to the point, the rise of these programs, especially their appeal to younger audiences, gives testimony to the inherent critical sensibilities of viewing audiences.

While viewers can be said to possess certain critical capabilities, these abilities are not uniformly held. Critical skills vary among age groups, education levels, and other demographic markers. Also, media forms are constantly changing. In the 2000s, the Internet created novel experiences and new social possibilities. Even as the economy has lumbered through recession, computer gaming stands as the fastest-growing area of the entertainment industry. And mobile technologies provide even greater access to all manner of movies, television programming, social networks, and virtual worlds that have grown more complex even as they have become more engaging.[8]

Imagined Communities

The historic rise of Twitter and Facebook transformed the term "social network" from an obscure academic reference into an everyday buzzword—and even the title of a popular film.[9] This duo of first-generation apps made good on predictions of a decade earlier about the potential of virtual communities—digital spaces for people to meet, chat, or simply develop a sense of togetherness. Of course, even at its most simplistic, a community is always more a relationship among people than it is a physical neighborhood or place. Long before the Internet came along, communities functioned as "networks" enabled by mail, phones, or other means. A few decades ago, Benedict Anderson succinctly explained that "the process of communication is in fact the process of community."[10] In Anderson's view, the very way that people see themselves as group members hinges on a conceptual leap uniting them, but this understanding is dramatically susceptible to suggestions by news and entertainment media. Anderson argues that even face-to-face communities exist partly in our minds, but, more generally, "communities are to be distinguished, not by their falsity or genuineness, but by the style in which they are imagined."[11] Recognizing the role of communication in community formation, linguistic scholars now speak of "speech communities" and "interpretive communities" in referencing how we are joined together by mental processes. All these groupings derive from understandings that generate a sense of inclusion and exclusion. In this regard, the notion of virtual communities, once considered a radical concept by Internet technophiles, is nothing new. To some the virtual community model offers little of consequence aside from the way it throws old ideas about community into relief. Manuel Castells writes that "the opposition between 'real' and 'imagined' communities is of little analytical use beyond the laudable effort at demystifying ideologies of essentialist nationalism."[12]

Considering how far we have come, the idea of communities made possible by the Internet seems rather obvious. But there is no denying the powerful effects that the "virtual community" exerts. And as with concepts like the cinematic gaze, we may not always be fully aware of how these effects work on us. In an era of mobile phones, wireless access, and proliferating e-commerce, it seems that almost all aspects of our lives have become digitized and thereby improved. But at the same time, might it be conceivable that digital connectedness resonates powerfully right now because so many people feel left out of or alienated by public life? Networked communities are not such a bad option when "real" communities are diminishing and so many people feel powerless. Is it merely a coincidence that Internet communities have exploded in popularity just as citizens are declining to participate in electoral politics, when corporate mergers and monopolistic business practices seem out of control, and when an idea as simple as universal health care generates intense political acrimony? Maybe the stage was already set for the Internet to bring us together.

Howard Rheingold, a famous cheerleader for the far-reaching potentials of "virtual" communities, wrote in 1993 about the possibilities of a life in cyberspace just like in the "real" world, except that "we leave our bodies behind."[13] To Rheingold, the disconnection between virtual and physical worlds was hardly worth worrying about: "Not only do I inhabit my virtual communities," Rheingold wrote, "my virtual communities also inhabit my life."[14] It is probably worth mentioning that this early technological utopianism typically ignored such nonvirtual inconveniences as hunger, poverty, bigotry, and violence.

These days live-chat technology has for many people supplanted formats like e-mail and Facebook. Once the exclusive province of business teleconferencing, now iChat and Skype bring interaction into real time for everyone. This capacity is particularly popular among kids below driving age, who can keep in touch with friends without ever leaving their rooms. This is hardly a casual change in human behavior. More than anything else, live-chat technologies bring "real" and "imaginary" communities together in a single realm. Instead of focusing on the discontinuities between virtual and nonvirtual worlds (in other words, representation and reality), we can view these two spheres as mutually informing. Each reflects and shapes the other. Perhaps we need not conceptualize virtual communities as ends in themselves so much as additional nodes of existing "spaces" of human dialogue and exchange.

The presumed separation of "real" and "virtual" worlds confuses understandings of how these two realms are in fact connected. Assertions discounting the "real" effects of "virtual" spaces can undervalue interrelationships between them, not to mention the very real material effects that virtual environments generate. We know that the Internet has become a prodigious medium of commerce. But often overlooked is how commerce capitalizes on our need for community in the way it develops and organizes cohorts of customers. Interactive capabilities built into Amazon's website enable the company to analyze information on purchases, generating a continually changing set of new product "recommendations." These seemingly friendly suggestions come with "customer reviews" from ostensibly like-minded purchasers. Amazon shoppers are supposed to get the impression they are members of a peer group with similar interests, forgetting that the suggestions are automatically generated by a database. Other merchandizers promote community with special gatherings, e-mail blasts, or print materials that compliment online retailing. Then there are member discounts, "priority" clubs, and preferred, or "prime," buyer groups. Every aspect of these supplementary plans intentionally suggests a sense of affiliation, loyalty, or "belonging" to something larger. Retailers know full well that people want this larger connection with others and that "communities of interest" have become an extremely effective means to build long-term customer relationships.

What does it mean when you can buy your way into a "community" for the price of a paperback? While this might sound harmless enough, such commodification of community has some unpleasant implications. How people form communities has a lot to do with how they understand themselves and how they engage others. It also says much about how and why people communicate. After all, it is through communication that human beings exchange information, find common meanings, and, ultimately, understand each other. This understanding is the source of our empathy and caring for one another. It makes the world a more compassionate and better place. When we turn community into a product, we move one step closer to viewing people in the same way. In other words, we move closer to seeing others as objects, as things, as less than human. And this is the very opposite of genuine community.

But don't tell this to the millions of people subscribed to eHarmony, the enormously successful matchmaking site launched in 2002 by psychologist Neil Clark Warren. In its first decade of operation, eHarmony overtook every other comparable online dating service to become a social force to be reckoned with. Combining a twenty-nine-point compatibility index with a client's dating preferences, eHarmony computers spit out matches intended to launch long-term relationships. And with over 30 million members, eHarmony claims that it now accounts for an astonishing 5 percent of all marriages in the United States.[15] In a world in which many adults find themselves increasingly frustrated by shrinking "real-world" social opportunities, most of us know at least someone who has used this kind of service.

Virtual communities also can have very real political effects, mobilizing letter-writing campaigns or demonstrations. The presidential elections in both 2008 and 2012 show just how important online political organizing has become, with both the Barack Obama and Mitt Romney campaigns expending tens of millions of dollars on social networking. On another level, virtual worlds project a material presence in the sheer economics of the companies involved. Aside from the debacle surrounding Facebook's initial public stock offering, Internet companies have proved an excellent investment opportunity for many. And then there is the use of the Internet as an advertising medium. Finally, as in the case of Amazon, the Internet enables a form of community building with the growing use of tracking and profiling to aggregate communities into mailing lists or databases for analysis. In this sense, practically everyone belongs to an online community, whether one knows it or not.

The imaginary character of currency has always made the economy a virtual affair. After all, money has always been a symbolic substance in the way it represents value. Without much public fanfare, huge sectors of the financial world have migrated even further into the virtual universe in the past decade. Practically all stock trading now takes place on the Internet—so much so that Wall Street has become worried that huge computer systems can easily manipulate stock prices.

With the relatively recent introduction of "flash trading," institutional investors now can execute millions of transactions in a few milliseconds. Small investors can find themselves blindsided by instantaneous blasts of money shot through the system from flash traders. Congress has begun to limit the power of virtual trading in an effort to minimize such occurrences.[16] This is but one way in which the entire financial system has become a virtual affair. While computer networks have made money transfers possible between banks for some time, the computer era has brought personal finance online as well, with automatic salary deposits and bill paying. Indeed, money has become much more ephemeral in our digital world.

And let's not forget digital games of chance. While online gambling remains largely illegal within the United States, virtual casinos and card rooms do a booming business from offshore network centers or Native American reservations with special waivers. While Congress remains divided about how to regulate online gambling, it continues to be against federal law for US financial institutions to handle such transactions.[17] Hence, online gamblers tend to use credit cards or bank accounts registered in other countries. Online poker rooms neatly illustrate two important characteristics of virtual experience: immersion and navigation. What could be more immersive than finding oneself at an online poker table and living with the very real financial consequences of one's actions? Enmeshed in a game of poker, gamblers find themselves in a quite specific world, with its own rules, strategies, and consequences. At the same time, this game experience affords one the ability to navigate the situation in an open-ended manner, choosing cards, placing bets, and so on. A person wins or loses what might seem like virtual money, but a very real transaction eventually takes place nevertheless.

There's just no getting around it. New media forms surround us, whether through movies and television or via online environments and games. Rather than worrying too much that these new digital domains are irrevocably transforming human consciousness, we would do better now to recognize how real and imaginary worlds coexist and mutually inform each other. There is no point in either clinging to old standards of communication or tossing them out in favor of new ones. The answer lies in recognizing continuities between what was and what can be.

Immersive Games

Virtual worlds remind us of the importance of games in human culture. In the second decade of the new millennium, electronic games now exist as the world's fastest-growing form of amusement. In 2005, the proportion of game players surpassed 50 percent of America's population.[18] By current estimates, the number of active computer gamers in the United States stands at 183 million.[19] Around the world, people now annually spend twice as much money on computer games as on movies. According to the Entertainment Software Association, adult game players spend seven hours per week engaged in the activity, and 84 percent of people playing electronic games are over the age of eighteen. Four out of every ten players are women, and a surprising 25 percent are over fifty years old.[20] In fact, the average player is thirty-five. Heads of households log into games at a rate of nearly 70 percent, with CEOs, CFOs, and other senior managers sneaking time at their desks at a rate of 61 percent.[21] In global terms, the world now spends over 3 billion hours per week playing some kind of computer game.[22]

Obviously computer games have become a huge economic force, with annual worldwide sales this year projected at nearly $70 billion.[23] The costs of developing and marketing a top game now surpass those for many feature films. This is hardly surprising, considering that games like *Wii Sports* (retailing for $29) and *Call of Duty* (retailing for $59.95) sold 80 million and 30 million copies, respectively, putting them on an economic par with the most successful Hollywood movies.[24]

The lure of computer games is no big mystery. While movies and television pull viewers into their worlds with imagistic clarity and the illusion of depth, games take matters a step further in allowing audiences to take control of the action within the virtual space. This makes for a powerful sense of inhabiting the virtual world. Everyone is familiar with accounts from concerned parents and others—not to mention gamers themselves—about the experience of becoming "lost" in game play and forgetting about time. Some even worry about game addiction.

The phenomenon of the virtual world in gaming has been brought to new heights in recent years with the growth of multiplayer role-playing games, most notably *World of Warcraft* (*WoW*). Such games maximize the virtual world experience by enabling players to assume the role of a character (usually a combatant) within the game space and to interact with others, either real-world friends or online acquaintances. Entire college dorm units play games like *Call of Duty* and *World of Warcraft* together, and networks of gamers are brought together by games. At times hundreds of players can inhabit the *WoW* game environment, which is so large that players can travel to towns, inhabit buildings, and roam across expansive terrains. Unlike earlier computer games sold as single-package software units, games like *WoW* are paid for via subscription. With over 9 million subscribers, *WoW* is estimated to hold over 60 percent of the multiplayer online game market.[25] As the name implies, *WoW* is a fighting game placing participants in an environment where they can potentially hunt, shoot, or blast hundreds of other players. But in the most popular multiplayer game, there is no fighting at all.

The Sims first appeared in 2000 as a game oddly seeming to lack a goal. Players simply assume an identity and construct a life for themselves in any of a variety of environments (homes, mansions, colleges, resorts, deserted islands), depending on the version of *The Sims* purchased. Initially a game for a single computer, *The Sims* became an online multiplayer experience in 2002. Since then, the nonviolent *Sims* has become the largest-selling game of them all, with over 100 million copies in circulation. Following on the success of *The Sims,* Electronic Arts launched a similar world-building game, *Spore,* which also has sold millions of copies. In *Spore,* players begin the game as a primitive organism that evolves over time into a creature, a community, and ultimately an entire planet of beings. Like other so-called God games, *Spore* encourages players to think about the interrelationships among creatures, communities, and the ecological sustainability of the worlds they ultimately come to create.

Spore is but one example of a new trend in game design. For years the computer game industry has sought ways to combat the perception of games as a waste of time. And it isn't just people selling games who tussle with this perception. What technology journalist Clive Thompson terms "gamer regret" is a concern among educators, parents, and, perhaps most importantly, gamers themselves. As Thompson puts it, "The dirty secret of gamers is that we wrestle with this dilemma all the time. We're often gripped by ... a sudden, horrifying sense of emptiness when we muse on all the other things we could have done with our game time."[26] The upshot of these worries is that the game industry is actively seeking ways to make games more positive, productive, and engaged with things that matter in the "real" world.

A research subculture examining the positive aspects of media and game culture has developed. For example, in *What Video Games Have to Teach Us about Literacy and Learning,*[27] James Gee takes a cautious look at the neurological processing skills that game technologies help develop. As the book's title indicates, Gee argues that computer games require certain types of skills unique to the game medium. Most obviously this entails a mastery of the game and its rules, which can be quite daunting. Anyone who has picked up a Sony PlayStation controller knows that it has no fewer than fifteen separate buttons and toggles requiring split-second dexterity to operate successfully. Games like *World of Warcraft* oblige players to animate their avatars using highly complex commands. Most uninitiated players find themselves hopelessly vulnerable when they start to play and are typically eliminated by experienced players within a minute or so. But this is only the beginning of the learning curve.

At the very least, it can reasonably be asserted that video games entail their own kind of "literacy"—like media literacy—that differs from spoken or written communication and has new and exciting applications beyond the theoretical realm. Some scholars have begun to write positively about the kinds of learning that video games foster. Gee argues that people assume roles in video games through which they learn about the world from different perspectives.[28] Although the "world" players experience generally is cartoonlike or violent, the experience can lead to useful insights, Gee asserts. For one thing, even in simple games, players often need to make subtle decisions. In the widely visited Neopets universe, participants as young as four or five years old choose up to four "pets" to own, nurture, and protect. Neopets players earn points, feed and even fight for their pets, and must decide which to favor and which to neglect—and possibly permit to expire (which also occurs if players ignore them for more than a couple days).

Central to the mental work of entering a virtual world—whether through a book, movie, television program, or computer game—is the engagement with an alternative universe. Reading any story means entering a narrative with its own rules, systems of logic, and vocabulary. The familiar Harry Potter books, movies, and games require readers to accept a world in which magical powers exist and operate in unique ways, with a hierarchy of institutions, professors, and master wizards. In fact, considerable comedy emerges in the interactions between the magical community and the world of "muggles" (nonmagical beings). Harry's Aunt and Uncle Dursley are muggles who are continually befuddled by a magical world they view as "not normal." The magical characters continually ridicule the pompously middle-class Dursleys, who simply are not privy to how the magical world works.

In interactive game environments, players must first assume an identity that conforms to others in the virtual world. To Gee, this entails a "committed learning principle" of gaining fundamental knowledge of the virtual world, as well as an "identity principle" that involves "taking on and playing with identities in such a way that the learner has real choices (in developing a virtual identity) and ample opportunity to meditate on the relationship between new identities and old ones."[29] Next, players begin the intellectual work of probing the virtual world, formulating hypotheses about how it operates and testing their ideas. Finally, life in the virtual world requires a tolerance for differences, a willingness to engage those one does not understand, and the ability to form communities with others.[30] It's worth acknowledging that all these skills have corollaries in the nonvirtual world. But they are exercised with an intensity and frequency in virtual game worlds quite different from other storytelling forms.

Game World Controversies

Not everyone is happy about our new game culture. For many adults computer games generate nothing but bewilderment and worry. Images come to mind of seedy pinball arcades, carnival sideshows, and growing up too quickly. And so many of the most popular computer games are indisputably violent—if not sexist and racist as well. As seen in movie, television, and music sales, the computer game industry moved quickly to establish its own ratings system with the Entertainment Software Rating Board, which in 1994 successfully headed off congressional efforts to regulate game content. All games now come labeled as "EC" (early childhood), "E" (everyone), "T" (teen), "M" (mature), or "AO" (adult only). But consumer advocates argue that weak enforcement of age restrictions on the labels has meant that stores routinely sell inappropriate games to youngsters anyway.

Attempts to criminalize the sale of adult-oriented computer games to minors began in 2005, with evidence that hidden scenes and erotic material in *Grand Theft Auto* could be unlocked with a software key found on the Internet. Suddenly mainstream political figures like Hillary Clinton (D-NY) and Rick Santorum (R-PA) jumped on the issue, sponsoring new laws to tighten controls over game content. But consensus proved impossible to achieve in a gridlocked Congress, and no such laws were ever passed. Much of this controversy was laid to rest—at least as relates to violence—by a 2011 Supreme Court decision striking down a California law criminalizing the sale of such video games to minors. In a 7–2 decision, justices deemed the law unconstitutional on free speech grounds. "No doubt a state possesses legitimate power to protect children from harm," said Justice Antonin Scalia, who wrote the majority opinion. "But that does not include a free-floating power to restrict the ideas to which children may be exposed."[31]

It remains a standing joke that none of the adult critics of computer games have ever tried playing one. As with earlier debates over media sex and violence, the testimony of "experts" continues to convince those concerned—but with a slight twist. Gamer critics worry that the active character of game play is far more seductive than the passive viewing of movies and TV. This reasoning was promoted most effectively by David Grossman, a retired military trainer and self-described "professor of killology."[32] In his highly influential book, *Stop Teaching Our Kids to Kill,* Grossman makes the point that computer games resemble combat simulators used in military training and that many in the armed services play "first-person shooter" games in their spare time.

Panic soon spread, despite a lack of any hard evidence, that games were transforming children into conditioned murderers. Of course, if anyone at the Pentagon was taking these claims seriously, the military might have stopped developing its popular video game *America's Army,* which has been used as a recruitment tool for over a decade. As one might expect, players in *America's Army* assume combat roles in which they fight, shoot, and blow a lot of things up. The *America's Army* website claims that since its inception, over 9 million players have become part of the *America's Army* experience, accounting for over 100 million hours of online combat "experience." This has earned *America's Army* the status of one of the top ten online action games and, until recently, the most popular war game in history.[33]

America's Army is so good that many active-duty soldiers prefer the game to commercial alternatives. To date, it seems that no one inside or outside the army has gotten confused about where the game ends and real fighting begins. But controversies about the game have surfaced nevertheless. As one critic explained, "It's one thing if the Army wants to use video games to desensitize soldiers so they can more easily kill 'the enemy.' But it's another thing to desensitize civilians in the same way, especially impressionable young people."[34]

Existing research on computer games has failed to clarify matters. Notable studies by Jeanne Funk, Derek Scott, and others couldn't prove a direct link between game play and increased levels of aggression, although Funk et al.'s study noted an increased tendency toward violence among children under age eleven whose "favorite" games featured fighting.[35] A comparative analysis rated the overall influence of computer games to be less than what derives from TV viewing.[36] While connections between game playing and aggression remain elusive, some researchers point to other problems. One study found that gamers are prone to higher levels of muscle strain and hypertension. Another said that gaming could be linked to obesity and poor academic performance.[37] At the same time, such findings are contradicted by researchers like Gregg Costikyan, who says that games can enhance certain problem-solving skills.[38] Others looking at games find they can quicken information processing.[39] One study even found that the diversion of virtual experience can reduce stress and help people cope with chronic pain.[40]

So which is it? Do video games teach kids to become violent or not? One thing is for certain: they do indeed impart to young people some computer-oriented skills, and they draw youngsters into them in the process. Otherwise they wouldn't work. In many games players must construct the characters—even in combat games—choosing from different costumes, attributes, and skills. This is especially the case in games like *Eve Online* or *RuneScape,* in which players enter fantasy environments inhabited by creatures like elves and gnomes. In the process, players must learn rules, formulate strategies, and make decisions affecting the well-being of others. But it's not as simple as simply choosing a wand or a hat. In many, this means working against menacing forces far more true to life than evil wizards. The now classic *Grand Theft Auto* situates itself in various urban centers in its different iterations, obliging players to work their way up criminal organizations. *Halo* centers on an interstellar war between humanity and a theocratic alliance of aliens known as the Covenant. *L.A. Noire* pays homage to 1940s and 1950s detective stories, placing gamers in a nostalgic, yet troubled, Los Angeles that can be traversed in color or black and white. Games like *Half-Life, Deux Ex,* and *Red Faction* pit contestants against powerful rich people or corporations. The *Battlefield* series portrays a variety of wars between the United States and other nations and rogue factions.

As these examples suggest, their requisite role-playing requires participants to place themselves in identities far removed from that of a typical suburban fourteen-year-old. Immersion in an imaginary universe heightens this experience. Some theorists argue that this act of imagining—and to some extent experiencing—a novel identity helps young people understand human difference and become more sympathetic toward people unlike themselves.[41] This position is countered by observations that shooting at police, urban minorities, or Muslims simply reinforces damaging stereotypes. For example, in the game *Ethnic Cleansing* players kill African Americans, Latinos, and Jews. Another potentially positive attribute of many games lies in the way characters frequently act in teams or mini-communities through which allies support each other and engage other groups.

Electronic games come in a number of media formats—from those sold in stores on CDs or DVDs to those accessed online. In some online games, players engage friends or acquaintances in the same room, dorm, or other limited network. Other games involve huge online communities of thousands of players.

One of the leading trends influencing the video game market is portable gaming, which continues to grow strongly. According to a recent study, 40 percent of video gamers are likely to purchase a portable gaming device in the next twelve months. And as of 2012, two out of every three smartphone owners regularly used their device for playing games.[42]

Many people concerned about media violence worry about the Internet as both a source of harmful content and a stalking ground for nonimaginary predators. Generally, most parents are concerned about sexual material, and their concern has successfully mobilized the industry to work on the problem. Web search engines like Google and Yahoo! come automatically set to filter out adult content so that young people can't accidentally call up pornography. (Any user can adjust the filters.) Commercial parental-control applications like Cybersitter, NetNanny, and SafeEyes similarly limit information computers can receive and simplify the process of monitoring what sites the computer accesses. But none of these safety measures do anything about violent content on the Internet. Hate groups like Aryan Nations and the Ku Klux Klan have long used the Net to recruit. Some white supremacist groups like Stormfront have created separate children's hate sites to entice youngsters. The strength of online hate sites lies in their ability to reach individuals who might be inhibited by fear of social embarrassment from buying printed materials or attending a hate group meeting. As with online pornography, the Internet allows people to view hate materials in the privacy of their homes. There really is no way to prevent people from finding violent imagery and expressions of hate on the Internet short of unplugging the computer. But with the accelerated growth of wireless gaming via cell phones and other smaller, more portable devices, the plug has become irrelevant.

Convergence Culture

Recently, the most popular gaming environments have started doing something that earlier games did not. Rather than situating the player as a lone combatant or adventurer, games like *World of Warcraft* and *Second Life* allow players to explore and "live" in a virtual space with others, resulting in a dramatic transformation of the game experience. Somewhat awkwardly abbreviated MMORPGs, these massively multiplayer online role-playing games have gained currency with advances in home computing and high-speed networks. Unlike games that reside on an individual computer, these newer games exist in "cloud" environments—

meaning that users log onto the games, which house data and functionality in their own servers. The new games require up-to-date graphics and media-processing capacities, but because their "worlds" are housed online, they consume little memory and can be run on newer, lighter devices like laptops, netbooks, or mobile phones. This, after all, is the future of personal computing anyway. The convergence of advanced microprocessing and high-speed networking has transformed people's relationship to their computer data, not unlike the way the advent of paper currency changed humanity's relationship to money and wealth. Rather than hiding boxes of gold in our homes, we store our money in a bank, where it is always accessible thanks to modern technology. As digital information becomes more and more a part of our lives, things like pictures and documents need a place to be stored—hence the metaphor of the cloud.

In the context of worlding, the new generation of MMORPGs represents a radical breakthrough in immersion, heightening the experience of inhabiting an alternative world unlike any previous popular media form. The full range of immersive experiences can only be fully appreciated by entering such a world. Trite as this phenomenological prescription might sound, it really is true. But the processes involved in the experience are not beyond explication. They simply resist reduction to language because so much seems to take place in games at the same time. Digital media theorist Henry Jenkins has written about this fact at length in *Convergence Culture: Where Old and New Media Collide*. To Jenkins, several phenomena are converging in contemporary media: the combination of previously separate media forms (graphics, sound, interactive technology), storytelling formats (books, TV programs, movies, games, toys), and media institutions (producing entities, distributors, networks). While "old media" could be pinned down to a few production formats or styles, the complex convergence that characterizes "new media" frustrates easy description.

Such analysis becomes even more difficult due to the phenomenon of immersion, the experience of "being inside" an imaginary world. By definition, immersion occurs when "the sensory experience of the actual world is sufficiently muted, and the sensory experience of the virtual world sufficiently heightened, so that persons feel they are no longer in the actual world."[43] In the new generation of MMORPGs, this immersion results from the simultaneous occurrence of three different experiences: media simulation, group immersion, and interdeterminacy.

Media simulation has already been discussed at length in this volume. Throughout history, human beings have sought to create convincing worlds by replicating reality or rendering engaging alternatives to it. From realistic impulses in Renaissance painting to the invention of photography, the human animal has moved ever closer to replicating the mental experience of apprehending the surrounding world. Movie special effects, 3-D technologies, Dolby sound, and virtual reality gadgets (helmets, goggles, theme park rides) have brought us ever closer to "reality"—or at least the forms of reality we typically associate with everyday experience. Media simulation in the new MMORPGs operates through vision, sound, and touch. The capabilities of consumer-grade computers and DSL networks both enable and limit the experience of online virtual experience. In terms of visual graphics, the games can approach, but never truly attain, photo-realistic rendering of people, animals, and plant life. Surfaces—often referred to as "textures"—are either digitally drawn or copied from photographic images. Human forms resemble the kind of partly realistic, partly cartoonish characters seen in movies. Due to the difficulty of rendering realistic human beings, many games like *World of Warcraft* and *Halo* feature plenty of imaginary creatures like dragons or elves as options for players to inhabit. But live animation compensates for any loss of detail in the visual makeup of a character. There is simply some-thing uncanny about navigating an avatar through a complex environment, a phenomenon dating to computer games emerging in the 1980s, like *Doom* and *Super Mario Brothers*. While the full range of physical motions and facial expres-sions is limited by the data stream, nevertheless the sensation of moving oneself through a world of other moving beings and elements contributes significantly to the immersive illusion. Here is the first example of how the convergence of several immersive elements makes the gaming experience greater than the sum of its parts. Players are willing to forgive cartoonish graphics or jerky avatar movements as they suspend disbelief and enter the immersive world.

Then add sound. While most online games still require players to type their spoken statements as texts or "chats," most games now have environmental sound channels through which dancing characters can hear music or visitors to a forest can hear birds chirping. And in recent years, live voice communication has become a part of many games in which players speak with each other much as they would on a cell phone or conference call. Interestingly, there has been a minor controversy over the introduction of live voice communication in some games. Does hearing a player's actual voice add to or detract from the illusion of being in another world, of being another person or creature? With this question in mind, game developers are beginning to offer simulators that allow players to alter their voices to match their characters or, perhaps more significantly, to protect their privacy.

Finally, there is no discounting the tactile element of gaming. Although this experience is limited most often to handling a computer mouse or similar device, the physical aspect of interacting with the computer is very powerful. Players literally come into contact with the game in this way, as bodily musculature and reflexes link mind, machine, and the virtual world. Aside from technical literature, very little has been written about the role of the tactile interface in connecting real bodies with virtual worlds. Yet anyone who has played these games knows what a vital function the physical interface serves. Just think about the importance of our hands and fingertips in our knowledge and experience of everyday life, as we come into contact with the form, texture, movement, and temperature of objects. Touching our world is every bit as significant as seeing or hearing.

Group immersion may well be the most important element in the new generation of online games. The experience of interacting and communicating in real time with multiple characters in a live and unfolding story sets the new immersive games apart from earlier so-called first-person games that simply placed the player in a world of automated others. Recognizing that others will hear and respond creates an immediate drama, even if the exchange is simply a chat about the weather. Many games employ a "role-playing" element in which one behaves toward others as one would in an imaginary story, requiring players to remain mindful of who and where they are. In his masterful study of virtual worlds, *Coming of Age in Second Life,* Tom Boellstorff asserts that social elements drive the immersive experience of new computer games; he observes that "the simultaneous presence of more than one person has been key to cultural understandings of virtual worlds."[44] Simply imagine that you are a character in a game based, say, on the *Twilight* book franchise, as rendered in iPod and iPad format by Summit Entertainment. You enter the world in the avatar of perhaps the perpetually forlorn Bella, and you speak to other characters, some of whom you may or may not know, as Bella would do in the familiar narratives. Others greet you as Bella, ask you about your day, and remember what you did yesterday, and before long you find yourself consumed with acting the part of Bella in a kind of improvisational theater, thinking of what Bella would do, what she would say, and how she would respond. At the same time, you are listening to others around you, considering their roles, and remembering your histories with each of them. Keeping track of all of this pulls you as a player into the immersive space on an imaginary level quite independent of graphic or sound elements. A powerful social dynamic occurs with the technical rendering of the game experience, giving it a potency that deepens over time.

Add to the group experience the elements of interpersonal relationship that accrue at different levels. Initially, most players of MMORPGs have the experience of being new and unskilled. There's no denying that finding one's legs in some of these games takes a bit of time and practice. Avatars don't move by themselves, and some maneuvers require complex button pushing, command statements, or knowledge of protocols. In combat games a lack of skill can be frustrating. Elsewhere it can simply provide opportunities to ask more experienced players for assistance. But the important point is that along the way to gaining skills, most players in the new immersive game pick up comrades, friends, or allies—as well as enemies in some contexts.

Indeterminacy drives both media simulation and group immersion. With the broad dispersion of high-speed Internet connections, the real-time experience of virtual worlds demands and holds one's attention, even if communication is done with a typed chat. You simply never know what's going to happen next—and this uncertainty imbues even the most banal encounters with a powerful sense of drama. On one level this can involve something as simple as keeping a conversation going. But in more complex game situations, players might have goals ranging from taking an online course to dragon slaying or from starting a romance to engaging in political activism. The key element of online game indeterminacy lies in the interaction among players in real time. This is a form of improvisational acting—making and creating a story in the moment in response to a given situation. And it constitutes another powerful experiential element of the immersive game.

Clearly MMORPGs evoke creativity. In essence, players are coauthoring a story as they interact. This generative element of the new gaming world contributes significantly to its potency. It taps into the creative energies that live inside everyone, awaiting a channel for expression. Online games provide an easily accessible and relatively safe way for people to pretend to be something or someone else in public, while writing a story for the avatar the player controls—but only to a point. And here is where the excitement lies, because one never really knows what will happen next. Will I prevail against the dragon? Will my new friend come back tomorrow? In this sense, indeterminacy brings the dimension of time into the new immersive gaming world. But unlike fairy-tale worlds that take players to an imagined past, the new immersive games offer worlds of a future yet to be experienced.

Massive Engagement

In the last five years, MMORPGs have begun to dominate the game world, due to their powerful immersive character. While not the biggest of these new multiplayer immersive games, *Second Life* is in many ways the most interesting from a creative and sociological perspective. Unlike nearly every other online game, *Second Life* is not based on a preexisting world with a set of rules and parameters. Instead, the developers of *Second Life* provide what is essentially a blank page of data space on which users and secondary game developers build and animate a wide variety of environments and options for play. *Second Life* users, who can obtain permanent accounts at no cost, simply begin with a self-selected human avatar and then set off to explore worlds of historical fantasy, urban drama, futuristic travel, or any of several hundred other choices—all completely driven by other *Second Life* users. In this way, *Second Life* and a few of its more recent imitators offer what is arguably the most diverse and democratic immersive game environment available. The game's unconstrained openness and invitation to user self-definition are part of why users often indeed speak of the game as their "second life."

As mentioned previously, *World of Warcraft* leads the MMORPG field. Following its launch in 2004 with an initial subscription base of 250,000, *WoW* has attracted 6 million players, each engaging with the game for an average of twelve to twenty-two hours per week. This amounts to an astonishing 5.93 million years of human consciousness in the *WoW* world.[45] By comparison, *Second Life* has 2 million subscribers. Conceptually, this fact alone is somewhat staggering, confronting the new *Second Life* player with the opportunity to jump into a sporting event crowded with spectators or a busy nightclub animated with dancing avatars—each one with a live human being tethered to it somewhere in the world. *Second Life* differs from other games, especially combat or quest-oriented ones, which tend to be male dominated. In *Second Life,* women make up nearly 60 percent of the user base, with many reporting that they value *Second Life* as a "safe space" to chat, make friends, and explore. As with many MMORPGs, the user community of *Second Life* is international, with non-US players outnumbering Americans by 10 percent. This adds yet another dimension to the worlding discussion, as the new multiplayer game environments, in essence, reconfigure the globe across national borders into new geographies and nationalities.

Perhaps the biggest difference between *Second Life* and many other games is the lack of a determining narrative or context. Creator Philip Rosendale consciously developed *Second Life* as a blank slate, an empty online data space where others could create their own stories or even businesses. As MIT professor Sherry Turkle puts it, "In a different genre, *Second Life* is a virtual 'place' rather than a game. Here, there is no winning, only living."[46] The self-defining aspect of one's experience and environment in *Second Life* is very important, signaling yet another turning point in the new dynamics of worlding. Simply put, we are talking about breaking down the age-old relationship between producer and consumer, between performer and audience, a relationship we have been conditioned to accept but perhaps don't actually enjoy. Writing recently in *Wired*, Michael Wolff interviewed dozens of people about the future of the Internet. Wolff discovered that both business people and theorists are beginning to agree that as the Internet has become a commonplace utility, we now tend to view it more as a tool than anything else. Rather than something you sit down and watch, it's something you pick up and use. As Wolff puts it, old media "imposed an unnatural behavior on its users—not the least of all a strict divide between creators and audience. The Internet, with a flat hierarchy, cheap distribution, and virtually no production barriers, lets people express themselves more naturally."[47] As Wolff concludes, "We're collaborative animals, it turns out, and joyful amateurs, interested more in entertaining and informing ourselves than in being entertained and informed by professionals."[48]

In her remarkable book *Reality Is Broken: Why Games Make Us Better and How They Can Change the World,* Jane McGonigal outlines several key motivating factors common to new massively multiplayer immersive game worlds: satisfying work, the hope of success, social connection, and a sense of something larger than ourselves.[49] A veteran of the game industry, McGonigal details the extent to which today's game developers study and draw on research in positive psychology to concoct techniques to draw players into their worlds and keep them engaged. As McGonigal writes, "Compared with games, reality is too easy. Games challenge us with voluntary obstacles and help us put our personal strengths to better use."[50] Recognizing that human beings are naturally social and task oriented, game developers carefully balance microchallenges with rewards that both individuals and fellow players can recognize. Rewards in the form of personal satisfaction and group approval accrue continually in the most successful games, as players accumulate points, conquer rivals, or enhance their worlds. McGonigal points out that players will readily face obstacles and even accept short-term failure because they know that if they persevere, an intrinsic reward is just around the corner. In this formulation the key ingredient isn't so much the accumulation of "things" or commodities as it is ego gratification or a sense of well-being. McGonigal writes,

Which rewards, exactly, are most essential to our happiness? My analysis of significant positive-psychology findings from the past decade suggests that intrinsic rewards fall into four major categories. First and foremost, we crave satisfying work, every single day. The exact nature of this "satisfying work" is different from person to person, but for everyone it means being immersed in clearly defined, demanding activities that allow us to see the direct impact of our efforts. Second, we crave the experience, or at least the hope, of being success-ful. We want to feel powerful in our own lives and ... like we're getting better over time. Third, we crave social connection ... [and] derive a large percentage of our happiness from spending time with the people we care about. We want to share experiences and build bonds, and we most often accomplish that by doing things that matter together. Fourth, and finally, we crave meaning, or the chance to be a part of something larger than ourselves.[51]

A great deal of theory has analyzed this kind of relationship between the culture and the self—as in the ways readers/viewers identify with stories and find personal meaning in books, movies, television programs, and the like. But in MMORPGs and other computer games, players are taking matters a step further by actively engaging the game space and other players in what must be described as a form of creative expression. Well before computer games came onto the scene, Paul Willis famously described the importance of what he termed "symbolic creativity" in the formulation of self-identity, even if that creativity entails such a seemingly banal and debased form of self-expression as consumer behavior.[52] To Willis, the ordi-nary pleasures of choosing what clothing to wear, preparing a meal, or building a personal music collection—activities so common in everyday culture—constitute significant building blocks in our conception of self and our perceptions of personal agency. Similarly, Raymond Williams asserted that the essence of culture is "ordi-nary," suggesting that our knowledge of our world and ourselves is grounded in the here and now of mundane daily experience. As we recognize the importance of everyday life and symbolic creativity, it is vital not to overromanticize consumer behavior as an authentic expression of some essential identity. Advertising and other kinds of media representation plant ideas that satisfy latent desires, as we all know. So the self, if we may call it that, often comprises various mental self-images that we collect and collage into the identity we present to the world. It is yet another form of collaboration we maintain with the world around us, an endlessly evolving tapestry of images, acquired experiences, and genetic baggage.

The key element in symbolic creativity, even if it is influenced by media sug-gestion, is that it is personally driven and can be an expression of self. Moreover, even a mediated perception of individual agency is a powerful thing. So in virtual game worlds, one chooses an avatar identity, with many players eventually expending enormous effort modifying and personalizing the little actor for which a life comes to be written. And here is the utopian dimension. Speak with almost any character in a virtual world about "real life" (RL), and the person behind the avatar typically will express that he or she is motivated to live a virtual life that exceeds what is possible in RL. Virtual experience becomes a kind of screen on which players project their desires, fantasies, and aspirations. It is the rare player in *Second Life,* for example, who fashions an avatar to look like the person behind the mask. More typically, players present themselves in the body they wish they could have—and that is just the beginning. Fantasies of power, adventure, and romance play out in a carnivalesque masquerade. Virtual worlds indeed offer a powerful escape from reality. But unlike old media, they offer a form of escape that is actively constructed by the player. This experience constitutes an important new way of modeling utopia.

But these worlds do more than simply document fantasies. Here again, collective immersion has an unexpected effect. In my experience, players often form mutual bonds, become "friends," and eventually begin to disclose aspects of their lives in the other world that is RL. In these conversations—and they are very common—people describe themselves with remarkable candor and self-criticality. In this context, individuals actually stand in the virtual world and "look back" at the RL version of themselves with a critical distance. In game worlds people describe themselves with a kind of dispassionate frankness that one rarely experiences in offline interactions. Owing to the general anonymity of virtual life, people open up about their real-life circumstances.

It's no secret that friendship is a powerful force in cyberspace. Online worlds can satisfy a desire for connection and generate a way of opening up to others in many instances. Before very long a simple "My job is terrible" conversation can evolve into deeper discussions of personal history, career plans, life aspirations—all described by the player as if the real-life self were a third person.

Such an ability to look back on oneself with a kind of critical distance may sound simple in the context of a game. But this self-distancing form of analysis and thought is a powerful tool in the realm of psychoanalysis. The term "mentalization" has gained currency in mental health parlance as a way of naming the ability to recognize one's own mental states and those of others. As a form of critical insight and self-consciousness, mentalization is a goal in some practices of psychotherapy. As articulated by Peter Fonagy, mentalization can serve as a form of imaginative mental activity that allows people to perceive and interpret human behavior in terms of intentional mental states (e.g., needs, desires, feelings, beliefs, goals, purposes, and reasons).[53] Put simply, mentalization entails both personal self-awareness and a capacity for empathy. This is not to suggest that immersive online worlds represent a therapeutic miracle. But one can assert that virtual worlds offer remarkable potentials for personal insight. These elements of online experience are barely being discussed at the present moment in academic discourse.

Virtual Living and the Real World

Earlier in this book I discussed the topic of utopia. While musings about a better world may emerge from the imagination, visions of utopia can be projected into the real world if an individual has the mind-set to believe they are possible. This is more than a casual choice on the individual's part, for it entails a transformation of the self—of the so-called subject—from a passive to an active state, a process of awakening that occurs through a realization, shift of consciousness, or recognition of empowerment. Henry A. Giroux has described the role of a "language of possibility" in such change.[54] The active subject reaches a point of release from the authoritarianism projected by society, government, school, or the workplace. Today the widespread longing for a language of possibility is palpable in the massive popular disenchantment with politics as manifest in popular media and daily life. The public yearns for a "something else" that it cannot name.

Throughout human history, authoritarianism has manifested in both overt and covert ways, whether through the brute force of totalitarian regimes or through the subtler machinations of contemporary liberal democracy. But authoritarianism inevitably produces a by-product that makes possible its undoing. It produces resistance that can be fostered and understood, nurtured and cultivated. Recognizing a language of possibility means realizing that people can change, that situations can be altered, that seemingly absolute control is never absolute. Power can be stripped away. But this is never an easy or automatic process. All the great emancipatory moments of our time have arisen only when a disempowered group has confronted oppression and inequality: the civil rights movements, peace and justice movements, recent struggles for equitable health care—all these resulted from the active choice of people to take back what they have lost. As Jacques Rancière has so eloquently pointed out, empowerment is not based on "given equality" but the active process of "doing equality."[55] This reclaiming of something lost takes more than a simple revolt against an immediate injustice. Lasting empowerment comes from the transformation of the self, a genuine process of "subject formation." To Rancière this results not merely in the exercise of power but in "a political relationship that allows one to think about the possibility of political subjectivity."[56]

Why does this change in subjectivity happen? How does a passive person become an active political being? Bell hooks speaks clearly about the desire for a "something else" in what she terms a "yearning": "'Yearning' is the word that best describes a common psychological state shared by many of us, cutting across boundaries of race, class, gender, and sexual practice. Specifically in relation to the postmodernist deconstruction of 'master' narratives, the yearning that wells in the hearts and minds of those whom such narratives have silenced is the longing for critical voice."[57] Hooks further describes a process she calls "coming to voice."[58] As the phrase implies, coming to voice refers to the moment when passive silence transforms itself into active speaking. This can mean anything—from voicing one's opinion over the lunch table, to writing a letter, to simply taking an action in one's life. "Voice" in this context is a metaphor for action, for self-awareness, and for agency to act.

Obviously computer games cannot guarantee radical changes in the way people think about their lives. But it seems that the experience of inhabiting virtual worlds offers some intriguing possibilities. To think in a new way, to actually change one's mind about something—this can occur as a result of a discussion or the kind of cultural experience that Northrop Frye described as the "educated imagination."[59] Evidence suggests that immersion in virtual worlds opens a doorway. For some the doorway is a simple escape to another place, perhaps a place of adventure or fun. But deeper immersion also permits an individual to partake in utopian imagination. Many players in virtual environments are fashioning the kind of world they wish they could have—with rules, characteristics, and relationships quite different from what they have in real life.

Is this substitute utopia a good or bad thing? Speaking somewhat theoretically, Berthold Brecht discussed the importance of such moments in terms of the transformative power of theater to rupture experience, to create a psychological "strangeness" that breaks open the mind and enables the possibility for something different to enter. It appears that virtual worlds embody this possibility. Traveling to a different reality allows one to look back on oneself and view oneself as in a mirror. This mirroring effect has been described by many writing about the mind, from Henri Wallon to Jacques Lacan. Suffice it to say that the mirror is part of the apprehension of the self in the world. We see ourselves in the mirror. We gain insight. We see the difference between the utopian worlds we imagine and the everyday world we know is real. Certainly, this is one important gift of virtual experience—not simply the escape to another place but the critical consciousness that we carry in our minds. Virtual experience can help us change how we think.

But is that all there is? Must we say that the best we can expect from virtual worlds is a change in attitude? The answer is a resounding no. The notion that no connection exists between real and imaginary worlds is part of the failed Enlightenment logic that would divide experience into neatly separated mind versus body. We now know that the brain is more than a manifestation of thought or soul. What we experience as human consciousness is in fact also the product of cells, enzymes, energy impulses, and all sorts of biochemical interaction. Moreover, games, movies, books, and other forms of cultural expression are "real" creations that human beings make. Even more importantly, they are also objects that cause people to think and act in both virtual and actual worlds. The question this raises is obvious. How do virtual experiences encourage us to act in the real world? Can games actually make us better people?

This much we do know: games are enormously popular, invite people to tackle challenging tasks, require extensive collaborative skills, and encourage sociability. As Jane McGonigal writes, "If we want to keep learning about how to improve our real quality of life, we need to continue mining the commercial game industry for these kinds of insights. The industry has consistently proven itself, and it will continue to be, our single best research laboratory for discovering new ways to reliably and efficiently engineer optimal human happiness."[60] An explosion has taken place in recent years in gaming for social purposes, encouraging players to think about the world outside the game. Today millions of people, young and old, are engaged with games that contribute astonishingly to their fellow human beings. The *Extraordinaries* and *GroundCrew* are two mobile phone games that connect people with needs with those willing to provide services or volunteer hours on a short- or long-term basis. The action of the games does not take place in cyberspace but in real-life situations and organizations to which players have been dispatched. *Folding@home* takes advantage of the untapped processing power in the Sony PlayStation 3 to enable scientists to work on protein-folding problems for Alzheimer's syndrome, cystic fibrosis, and cancer research. User-donated distributed time on 1 million PlayStation 3 units on six continents now accounts for 74 percent of the computing in the *Folding@home* effort. *Free Rice* is a game in which players win actual food donated to the nonprofit organization

FreeRice.com. So far, *Free Rice* has provided over 10 million meals to hungry people worldwide. In *EVOKE,* players engage their local communities by devising strategies in which each player permanently increases the food security of at least one person. *World without Oil* asks players to imagine scenarios of energy depletion and to conceive solutions.[61] Even the children's MMORPG Club Penguin now has a philanthropic component through which 3 million players have contributed to humanitarian causes worldwide.[62]

McGonigal writes, "Alternate reality games are reinventing our real-life experience of everything from commercial flying to public education, from health care to housework, from our fitness routines to our social lives. We've seen how these games can help us enjoy our real lives more, instead of feeling like we want to escape from them."[63] This is not to suggest that all virtual worlds or virtual experiences do this. As always we must be careful not to overromanticize the potentials of the Internet, games, or any new technology.[64] But at this point in our history, it is fair to say that a turning point has been reached in virtual worlds. A real potential exists for such an intellectual change. However, the kind of growth that is possible takes some effort on the part of the user. To put it simply, it takes some education. Mindless wandering through *World of Warcraft* or *Spore* won't by itself teach us anything. But if one is willing and ready to contemplate one's realities, great things are possible. Enabling this understanding is the purpose of this book. And this can be the task of each of us, to set forth to promote dialogue in our lives. We need not look to huge institutions and governments to make changes in our world. We can begin in the smallest and seemingly least significant places—with friends, at home, in school, or in the workplace. In these everyday places we can promote possibility, we can share with others, and we can build the dream of a better world together.

Notes

1. Rachel Kaplan and Stephen Kaplan, *Cognition and Environment: Functioning in an Uncertain World* (New York: Praeger, 1982).

2. Stephen Kaplan, "Environmental Preference in a Knowledge-Seeking, Knowledge-Using Organism," in *The Adapted Mind: Evolutionary Psychology and the Generation of Culture,* ed. Jerome Barklow, Leda Cosmides, and John Tooby (New York: Oxford, 1992).

3. Jay Appleton, *The Experience of Landscape* (New York: Wiley, 1975).

4. Denis Dutton, *The Art Instinct: Beauty, Pleasure, and Human Evolution* (New York: Bloomsbury, 2009), 21.

5. Christian Metz, *Film Language: A Semiotics of Cinema,* trans. Michael Taylor (New York: Oxford, 1974).

6. Laura Mulvey, "Visual Pleasure and Narrative Cinema," *Screen* 16, no. 3 (Autumn 1975): 6–18.

7. Ferdinand de Saussure, *Course in General Linguistics,* trans. Wade Baskin (London: Fontana/Colins, 1974).

8. Steven Musil, "Video Games Sales Revenue Plummets 31 Percent," CNET News, July 16, 2009, http://news.cnet.com/8301-10797_3-10289207-235.html (accessed August 17, 2011).

9. *The Social Network,* directed by David Fincher, written by Aaron Sorkin (Columbia Pictures, 2010).

10. Benedict Anderson, *Imagined Communities: Reflections on the Origin and Spread of Nationalism* (London: Verso, 1983).

11. Ibid., 6.

12. Manuel Castells, *The Information Age: Economy, Society, and Culture, vol. 2: The Power of Identity* (London: Blackwell, 1997), 29.

13. Howard Rheingold, *The Virtual Community: Homesteading on the Electronic Frontier,* revised ed. (Cambridge, MA: MIT Press, 2000), 3.

14. Ibid., 10.

15. "Eharmony," The Internet Dating Guide, www.theinternetdatingguide .com/2007/10/eharmony.html (accessed August 17, 2011).

16. Karey Wutkowski, "U.S. Regulators Propose Ban on 'Flash' Trading," Reuters, September 17, 2009, www.reuters.com/article/2009/09/17/us-sec-flashtrading-idUSTRE58G6KP20090917 (accessed September 18, 2011).

17. Dan Goodwin, "US Lawmakers Renew Fight for Legal Online Gambling," *The Register,* May 26, 2009, www.theregister.co.uk/2009/05/26/online_gambling_bill (accessed August 16, 2011).

18. "Facts and Research: Game Player Data (2005)," Entertainment Software Association, www.theesa.com/facts/gameplayer.asp (accessed May 3, 2010).

19. Jane McGonigal, *Reality Is Broken: Why Games Make Us Better and How They Can Change the World* (New York: Penguin, 2011), 2.

20. "Facts and Research" (accessed October 5, 2010).

21. McGonigal, *Reality Is Broken,* 8–9.

22. "The Business of Media Violence," Media Awareness Network, www.media-awareness.ca (accessed May 3, 2010).

23. Ibid.

24. "Call of Duty: Modern Warfare III," Global Weekly Chart, VGChartz.com, www.vgchartz.com/game/44606/call-of-duty-modern-warfare-3/Global/ (accessed January 10, 2012).

25. Mike Fahey, "*World of Warcraft*'s U.S. Sales Numbers Are Massive," Kotaku, http://kotaku.com/5325771/world-of-warcrafts-us-sales-numbers-are-massive (accessed August 16, 2011).

26. Clive Thompson, "Battle with Gamer Regret Never Ceases," *Wired,* September

10, 2007, www.wired.com/gaming/virtualworlds/commentary/games/2007/09/ gamesfrontiers_0910 (accessed July 20, 2011).

27. James Gee, *What Video Games Have to Teach Us about Literacy and Learning* (New York: Palgrave, 2003).

28. Ibid.

29. Ibid., 67.

30. Ibid., 90.

31. "Supreme Court Violent Video Games Ruling: Ban on Sale, Rental to Children Unconstitutional," *Huffington Post,* June 28, 2011, www.huffingtonpost .com/2011/06/27/supreme-court-violent-video-games_n_884991.html (accessed July 20, 2011).

32. David Grossman and Gloria DeGaetano, *Stop Teaching Our Kids to Kill* (New York: Random House, 1999).

33. America's Army, www.americasarmy.com (accessed July 20, 2011).

34. Brad Bushman, "Army Video Game Breeds Violence with Tax Money," *Detroit News,* May 9, 2004, www.detnews.com/2004/editorial/0405/09/a13-146738.htm (accessed September 1, 2010).

35. Jeanne B. Funk et al., "Rating Electronic Games: Violence in the Eye of the Beholder," *Youth and Society* 30, no. 3 (1999): 283–312; Derek Scott, "The Effect of Video Games on Aggression," *Journal of Psychology* 129 (1995): 121–132.

36. J. L. Sherry, "The Effects of Video Games on Aggression: A Meta Analysis," *Human Communications Research* 27 (2001): 409–431.

37. C. A. Phillips et al., "Home Video Game Playing in School Children: A Study of Incidence and Patterns of Play," *Journal of Adolescence* 18 (1995): 687–691.

38. Gregg Costikyan, "The Problem of Video Game Violence Is Exaggerated," in *Video Games,* ed. R. Espejo (San Diego, CA: Greenhaven, 2003), 27–34.

39. R. D. Health, "Video Games and Your Vision," *Reader's Digest* 163 (2003): 190.

40. Beyond Online Limited, "Video Games Can Be Used for Therapeutic Purposes," in *Video Games,* ed. R. Espejo (San Diego, CA: Greenhaven, 2003), 65–68.

41. Gee, *What Video Games Have to Teach Us,* 151.

42. "Mobile/Portable Gaming: Market Updates," Parks Associates, www .parksassociates.com/blog/article/parks-pr2011-mobilegaming (accessed October 18, 2012).

43. Tom Boellstorff, *Coming of Age in Second Life: An Anthropologist Explores the Virtually Human* (Princeton, NJ: Princeton University Press, 2008), 112.

44. Ibid.

45. Statistics on *WoW* in this section are from McGonigal, *Reality Is Broken,* 52.

46. Sherry Turkle, *Alone Together: Why We Expect More from Technology and Less from Each Other* (New York: Basic Books, 2011), 158.

47. Michael Wolff, "The Web Is Dead: Long Live the Internet," *Wired,* August 17, 2010, www.wired.com/magazine/2010/08/ff_webrip/all/1 (accessed July 21, 2011).

48. Ibid.

49. McGonigal, *Reality Is Broken.*

50. Ibid., 17.

51. Ibid., 51–52.

52. Paul Willis, *Common Culture: Symbolic Work at Play in the Everyday Cultures of the Young* (Boulder: Westview Press, 1990).

53. Peter Fonagy, *Affect Regulation, Mentalization, and the Development of the Self* (New York: Other Press, 2005).

54. Stanley Aronowitz and Henry A. Giroux, *Education Under Siege: The Conservative, Liberal, and Radical Debate over Schooling* (South Hadley, MA: Bergin and Garvey, 1982).

55. Jacques Rancière, quoted in Todd May, *The Political Thought of Jacques Rancière: Creating Equality* (University Park: Pennsylvania State University, 2008).

56. Jacques Rancière, "Ten Theses of Politics," *Theory and Event* 5, no. 3 (2001), http://muse.jhu.edu/login?auth=0&type=summary&url=/journals/theory_and_event/v005/5.3ranciere.html (accessed September 26, 2012).

57. Bell hooks, "Postmodern Blackness," *Postmodern Culture* 1, no. 1 (September 1990): 25.

58. Ibid.

59. Northrop Frye, *The Educated Imagination* (Bloomington: Indiana University Press, 1964).

60. McGonigal, *Reality Is Broken,* 346.

61. Games in this section are described at length in McGonigal, *Reality Is Broken.*

62. "Club Penguin," Wikipedia, http://en.wikipedia.org/wiki/Club_Penguin (accessed January 12, 2012).

63. McGonigal, *Reality Is Broken,* 347.

64. Turkle, *Alone Together.*

CHAPTER SEVEN
THE MEAN WORLD

Worlds can be scary places, whether real or imaginary. In this respect, the two kinds of worlds interact in serious ways. In the physical world of people, commodities, and nations, the human condition often leads to disagreement, conflict, and violence. In the nonphysical world of stories, media, and virtual encounters, narratives of discord and its consequences seem to dominate discourse. Just think about everyday existence and escalating anxieties in the post-9/11 era. Our worries start with everyday experiences and what we are told about them. From the minute you wake up in the morning, you are bombarded with reasons to worry. Get out of bed and go into the bathroom. Every product has a warning label; even swallowing too much mouthwash has potentially fatal consequences. Choosing what to eat for breakfast reminds us that many foods cause weight gain, contribute to illness, or contain harmful ingredients. Dressing for the day, you hear that the economy is slowing down, interest rates are rising, and the terror alert level has been raised. Heading out the door, you set the security alarm, then walk to your car and turn off that alarm. Getting into the car you glimpse yourself in the rearview mirror and realize that you are alone.

Our daily worlds envelop us with a culture of fear—not simply a fear of immediate danger but also a broader fear that we're doing something wrong or that we aren't all that we could or should be. These feelings are no accident. Nor are they in any way a natural part of us. They enter our experiential world from elsewhere. They come from our friends, family, and the media. Ironically, we get them from some of the people and things we really like. That's why they work. On a conscious level, we are aware that our immediate surroundings, the things we consume, and broader world we inhabit are all fraught with dangers. We can minimize these dangers by knowing where they lurk, being smart about how we live, and protecting ourselves and our loved ones in every way we can. But safety comes with a price. To feel secure we alter how we act, make compromises in what we want to achieve, and pay—on many levels—for a perception of safety. We do whatever is necessary to protect our health, we buy whatever products or services will help us look good and integrate successfully into society, and we support a legal system and legislature that will act on our behalf to protects us, using violent means—even killing other people—if necessary.

The Mean World Syndrome

The culture of fear creates what veteran media scholar George Gerbner has called the "mean world" syndrome—the belief that our world is a dangerous place where movie-style heroes and villains really exist and violent force is necessary to sustain our ongoing well-being.[1] This makes fear a part of our identity. Stemming from more than an occasional scare from a horror movie or a phobia about germs, anxiety takes over our sense of who we are and who we might become. People experience so many anxieties in so many aspects of life that a feeling of fear starts to control them and their society. Much news and entertainment is driven by stories that produce fear, and many of the consumer products we buy are purchased to ward off various insecurities and anxieties.

Where does such thinking come from? Why does such anxiety color our experiential world in the absence of verifying evidence or logical inquiry? The answer is that collective fear is a mental attitude driven by money and sustained by social anxiety in an era of growing uncertainty. In recent years a number of well-researched books have discussed our skittish culture. Barry Glassner's *The Culture of Fear: Why Americans Are Afraid of the Wrong Things* largely criticizes hyperbolic news and entertainment media for frightening people.[2] David L. Altheide's *Creating Fear: News and the Construction of Crisis* discusses what he terms "the problem frame" that "promotes a discourse of fear that may be defined as the pervasive communication, symbolic awareness, and expectation that danger and risk are a central feature of the effective environment."[3] Wole Soyinkka's *The Climate of Fear: The Quest for Dignity in a Dehumanized World* says anxieties once focused on nuclear annihilation now attach themselves to other ideas, especially in the post-9/11 years.[4] Corey Robin's *Fear: The History of a Political Idea* addresses concerns about international conflict and potential attacks on civilian populations.[5]

It's important to stress that despite the cloud of confusion in the public generated by post-9/11 media, these broad social anxieties were well in place before those events. In 1999 Zygmunt Bauman eloquently wrote of the growing mood of "uncertainty, insecurity, and unsafety" in contemporary society.[6] Increasingly people feel abandoned by public institutions and deceived by corporations. The majority hate their leaders yet never vote. Some would call this a postmodern moment in which the monolithic certainties of a prior era have been thrown into question. As once dominant formulations of male authority and the nuclear family give way, the nation-state is undermined by the rise of multinational capitalism. Media narratives of a fantasized return to origins soothe the anxieties produced by these changes.

Think about all the reasons people have to be disillusioned with and worried about once stable public symbols. Here real-world events color our experience. From America's failure in Vietnam, to Nixon's resignation, to the Reagan administration's Iran-Contra scandal, to the exploits of Bill Clinton and George W. Bush, to disappointments with Obama, people have lost faith in the presidency for good reason. Then there are the shenanigans of a host of other (mostly former) politicians: Rod Blagojevich, Larry Craig, Arnold Schwarzenegger, Eliot Spitzer, and Anthony Weiner. Religion hasn't fared much better, with sex scandals in the Catholic Church and the hysteria of US religious hard-liners. Corporate misbehavior and greed have reached such proportions that Congress, after much arm-twisting, passed the Sarbanes-Oxley Act to throw CEOs in jail. Celebrities haven't fared well either. Consider Christina Aguilera, Lindsay Lohan, Charlie Sheen, and a host of other less pious public figures exposed for vices ranging from drug abuse to lewd behavior. It's been a sad time for role models.

Then there is the economy and its effect on real and imaginary worlds. The recession has taken its toll, and the long-term outlook isn't good. Average Americans don't need to be told that their money is buying less, good jobs are harder to find, and much of what they put on their backs, drive, and listen to is made in the growing economic powerhouses overseas. As the gap between rich and poor continues to widen in Western nations, countries in Africa and parts of Asia and Latin America fall further into misery and despair. And it isn't someone else's problem when billions of people are hungry and diseased. Extremist factions in these nations are growing increasingly angry about the global imbalance in power and resources. Although the United States and its allies may say that they don't believe it, desperate people around the world hoping for a day of reckoning are finding common cause in their hatred for nations that callously exploit the rest of the world. After all, that was the real message delivered by the bombings in New York, London, Spain, and scores of lesser-known locations throughout Iraq, Afghanistan, and other nations. People in industrialized nations have every reason to be nervous that the intensity of such attacks will only increase as their governments continue to ignore the reasons they occur.

All of this emerges from the changing character of international conflict and war in the 2000s. Vietnam taught the United States about the difficulties of fighting insurgent enemies on their home turf. The Vietnam conflict handed the United States its first widely recognized defeat in the post–World War II era. Since Vietnam, US military adventures have become even messier as America has sought to protect its interests and head off future violence. The messiness comes with the difficulty of trying to combat enemies we can't always define as nations. We know that al-Qaeda is an ideological movement with cells throughout the Middle East, Asia, Europe, and elsewhere. And in the nations where al-Qaeda flourishes—like Afghanistan, Pakistan, and Yemen—it often operates as a minority guerilla movement rather than a national force. This causes confusion in our foreign combat missions and disagreement within the United States over how we deploy troops and treat those we capture. Hence, world boundaries continue to blur in our minds.

Shock and Awe

Many people blame our culture of fear on violence in the media. The topic of media violence has motivated much of the debate over broadcast public policy for several decades. At the same time, media violence remains one of the most widely discussed, yet least understood, issues of our time. The ubiquity of violent imagery in everyday life makes it a topic about which everyone has an opinion. Yet the fractured and contradictory character of the public debate on media violence offers little insight. Instead, the discussion degenerates into arguments between those who fear and those who relish such material. Lost in these discussions are considerations of why violent representations are so common and how they satisfy certain audience desires. Also largely missing are discussions about the various stakeholders in the media-violence debate: consumers, industry producers, child advocates, academic media "experts," outraged politicians, and journalists covering the issue.

Efforts to study the effects of violent media have proven more challenging than one might assume. In one notorious study conducted early in the television era, a group of US researchers were convinced they could measure the effects of violent media if they could eliminate other influences.[7] Researchers thought that a confined population—like prison inmates or hospital patients—might be just what they needed. In this instance, the study was conducted on boys living in boarding schools where TV habits were tightly regulated. For over a month, 50 percent of the boys were allowed access only to nonviolent programs, while the rest were permitted to watch anything they wanted. The expectation was that the students watching nonviolent shows would be better behaved, as had been demonstrated in studies of younger children. But what happened surprised everyone. As time passed, the kids watching nonviolent shows began acting up, using foul language, assaulting each other, and even committing acts of vandalism. Meanwhile the cohort that was free to watch violent programming remained compliant and studious.

The researchers struggled to figure out what had happened. Could it be that violent shows had helped viewers blow off steam? This assertion certainly wasn't backed up by past studies of the so-called catharsis effect, which consistently had been disproven. After a more systematic examination of the situation, the researchers arrived at a startling conclusion: the students restricted to nonviolent programs had reacted badly because they missed their favorite shows. Access to what they enjoyed watching, it turned out, had a much bigger influence on boys' attitudes than the amount of violence they saw.

It's important not to overstate the case made by this single study. Plenty of research has accumulated over the past decade showing the harm violent media can cause. But the risks are not always as obvious as they might at first appear. Assumptions one might make based on observing a four-year-old throwing a kick like a cartoon character may not be valid when applied to a teenager, a six-year-old, or even another preschooler. As with the children in the boarding schools, media affects its viewers in highly variable and individualized ways. Similarly, aggression and criminal behavior are influenced by far more than violent media. Despite assertions by anxious politicians and well-intentioned mental health professionals that social problems might be ameliorated with healthier television-viewing habits or less time with a game controller, opinions among academics, educators, and policy makers have gradually shifted in recent years toward a more holistic view of what causes violence in our society.

Understanding the issue of media violence requires an approach that goes beyond simple arguments of condemnation or support. In questioning typical views of media violence, it is important to view the topic in a broader context—taking into account the social, economic, and political factors that encourage and thrive on violent entertainment. Also worth consideration are the uses that violent stories play in education, art, and historical accounts of war, genocide, and violence stemming from natural catastrophes. In addition, one should examine the distinctly American style of much media violence. Historically the United States dominated global media production and was the source of most of the movies and television shows the world saw. The picture changed somewhat when multinational corporations began restructuring production and distribution in the 1980s and 1990s, but the influence of US television and moviemaking has endured even in the face of burgeoning media industries in other nations.

Beginning with a look at history, one should consider concerns about violent media that have accompanied the development of new communications media, from the printing press to the Internet. Different stakeholders in the media-violence debate—audiences, producers, and academics—have often viewed the topic in mutually exclusive, one-dimensional terms. One might ask why, in the face of so many efforts to curb the proliferation of violent material, media violence continues to escalate in new and more potent forms. Answering this question requires asking why media violence exists and how we can learn to deal with it.

Suspicions about the purportedly negative effects of violent representations on day-to-day behavior emerged well before the advent of film and television media. Street performances and dime novels were thought to erode the morals of the working poor, especially the growing populations of young men in cities. Looking back even further in history, both Aristotle and Plato commented on the public risks associated with stories about fighting and conflict. Given the long-standing character of these concerns, any serious consideration of media violence should begin by identifying continuities over time in public worries about such material. We also need to consider the quite different ways that media convey their violent content. Questions need to be posed about how the discourse on violent representation could remain so riven with inconsistency through so many decades of public debate and intellectual scrutiny. While plenty of researchers continue to maintain that violence in media is harmful, solid arguments have failed to materialize about just why this is so. In no small measure, this results from problems in reaching any consensus about what we mean by the term "media violence."

Witnessing Violence

Media violence means different things to each of us. Mention the phrase, and most people have no trouble calling to mind a brutal news clip, horror film, or graphic video game. But can we say that media violence is limited only to depictions of physical harm? Does psychological torment count? Do intentions or consequences count? How about accidents or acts of nature? What about verbal assaults or threats? Can we say there are degrees of violence? Is justified violence more acceptable than irrational acts? What about violence in comedy or the socially sanctioned violence of sports? How about historical documentaries or the evening news?

Let's face it: violent depictions are deeply ingrained in our culture. Throughout human history violence has figured prominently in storytelling. Such themes appear consistently in classical mythology throughout the world, as well as literature and the fine arts, folklore, and children's stories. Canonical texts like the Bible, the Torah, and the Koran use aggression and conflict to convey moral lessons. Fairy tales warn kids about the menacing consequences of disobeying adults. Classical paintings and public memorials offer up reminders of wars and battles. What can we say about violence in the current era? Removing violence from home entertainment is considerably easier now that TVs have the V-chip. But what would be the consequence of eliminating violence from popular programming? If we rid ourselves of offerings like *Fear Factor* and *World War Z* (2012) simply on the basis of violence, that criterion would apply as well to films like *Saving Private Ryan* (1998), *Schindler's List* (1993), and *Hotel Rwanda* (2004)—not to mention children's favorites from *The Lion King* (1994) to *Harry Potter and the Deathly Hallows* (2010–2011).

Certainly violent representation has become a staple of everyday life, and the volume of such material keeps growing. Anyone reading a newspaper or turning on a TV will find some form of violent imagery. Like the war on drugs and the war on terrorism, our long-standing campaign to stem the tide of media violence has failed miserably. In scientific terms, quantitative studies of violence have tended to focus on television, where the number of violent events can be calculated relative to total programming. By some estimates a young person will witness as many as two hundred thousand simulated violent acts before finishing high school.[8]

Researchers have tried to formulate "objective" definitions in their quest to measure media violence. In the 1960s and 1970s, this simply meant counting how many times a character threw a punch or shot a gun, with incidents in dramas and comedy shows receiving the same weight. No attempt was made to draw distinctions between realism, fantasy, or comedy until the 1980s, when analysts began to consider the realism or consequences of violent depictions, as well as the psychological implications of aggression. The turning point came in the mid-1990s, when several well-respected universities conducted the National Television Violence Study (NTVS), analyzing thousands of hours of broadcast material. Studying twenty-three network and cable channels, the NTVS found that children and adults watched three to four hours of television each day, potentially witnessing nearly twenty thousand violent acts each week.[9] Not much has changed since then. Violence is seen on a daily basis by people of all ages. Besides the violence regularly appearing on television dramas, sports, and Saturday morning cartoons, the public's sense of immediacy and realism in televisual violence has been heightened even further by journalistic accounts of war and terrorism. Add to this the rise of reality-based programs and the message is clear: the mediascape is becoming a much more violent place.

But the NTVS did more than simply count violent incidents. It was the first major study to take context into consideration. In doing so, the NTVS reached the startling conclusion that "not all depictions of violence are harmful."[10] There is a difference between violence presented graphically and that which is simply implied. The NTVS said that one has to take into consideration what type of character commits the violence, for what purpose, and what consequences result. Does a hero or villain commit the violence? Is the action punished or rewarded? Does the violence hurt anyone? In many programs such depictions seem to have no effect whatsoever, as in much comedic and cartoon violence. Does the program suggest we should feel empathy for the victim? Finally, can we discern the intended audience for the program? Not all people react to violent material in the same way, the NTVS asserted. In this crucial sense, not all media violence is created equal. These distinctions and nuances hitherto had been missing from public debates over media and its effects.

Much of what we see today in movies and on television is enhanced by digital technology. Computerized special effects do more than offer up attention-getting pyrotechnics. They blur the line between reality and fantasy in ways we don't always recognize. While the quantity of gore in today's movies may be comparable to that brought to us in the 1990s, the technical means by which violence can be seen and imagined has grown ever more sophisticated. Science fiction films like *Battleship* (2012) and *Catching Fire* (2013) introduce new kinds of blasters, phasers, and aliens, while horror films like *Breaking Dawn* (2012) and *Abe Lincoln: Vampire Hunter* (2012) suggest that vampires and other killers can materialize just about any time from thin air. A spate of war films like *Brave* (2012), *Post Mortem* (2012), and *GI Joe: Retaliation* (2012) use digital technology to bring thousands of combatants to the screen, as have fantasy movies like the *Iron Man* trilogy (2008–2013). Popular imports like *Tsotsi* (2006) and *The Flowers of War* (2011) have vividly portrayed massive human carnage, and computer effects have allowed martial arts films like *The Kick* (2012), *Monkey King* (2012), and *The Raid* (2012) to launch physical combat into supernatural dimensions.

Many people will argue that media violence simply satisfies a human desire for dramatic storytelling. Anthropologist Karl Lorenz argued fifty years ago that primitive instincts drive people to seek out stimulating narratives.[11] Media scholar George Gerbner coined the term "cultivation theory" to describe the way that viewers become acclimated to certain types of representation, especially those that heighten the intensity of what they are viewing.[12] Dolf Zillman has made similar assertions. But do people actually prefer violence to its alternatives? Or are audiences simply responding to what is most available? Often unacknowledged in the violence debate is the statistical fact that TV comedies and game shows routinely attract larger audiences than violence-ridden dramatic offerings.

Violence has always figured prominently in storytelling. Worlds of violence have been around since hunters began scratching accounts of their exploits on the walls of caves. Whether or not one believes that violent behavior is an innate part of human nature, violence has always played a major role in storytelling. Artifacts of Egyptian, Sumerian, Minoan, and Babylonian peoples all depict violent events, as do classical works of the ancient Greeks written three thousand years ago. All rely on violence to propel their narratives. Homer's *Iliad* (c. 760 BCE) relentlessly recounts military conflict, assassination, mass execution, sexual assault, and natural disaster. The same holds true for the *Odyssey* (c. 680 BCE), Hesiod's *Theogony* (c. 700 BCE), Aeschylus's *Oresteia* (c. 458 BCE), Sophocles's *Oedipus the King* (c. 428 BCE), and Thucydides's *History of the Peloponnesian War* (c. 424–440 BCE). The books of the Old Testament, written during the same period, are filled with accounts of genocide, war, human sacrifice, and, of course, various plagues. And as Mel Gibson so eloquently reminded moviegoers with his hugely successful film, *The Passion* (2004), the biggest story of the New Testament culminates in rioting, ritual torture, and public execution. Perhaps more to the point, these grizzly stories have been repeated for centuries to children and adults alike as important works of history and religion.

The pattern continues in the centuries to follow, suggesting that violent worldviews are deeply embedded in the types of stories Western civilization tells itself. Literary works of the Middle Ages like Dante's *Inferno* (1302) and Chaucer's *Canterbury Tales* (1386–1400) are riddled with detailed descriptions of violent assault and death. The best-known plays of William Shakespeare, including *Hamlet* (1607), *Julius Caesar* (1600), *Macbeth* (1606), *Othello* (1605), and *Romeo and Juliet* (1595), rely heavily on patricide, fratricide, suicide, and plain old murder to drive their plots. These works by Shakespeare were, in their day, the cultural equivalents of *Modern Family* and *CSI*. Everybody saw them, from the illiterate "groundlings" who sat on the floor of the public theater to university-educated elites and those who might attend special performances at Queen Elizabeth's court.

The printing press enabled dissemination of violent views of the world beyond the stage. Gutenberg's invention of moveable type in 1452 and the subsequent development of vellum paper meant that by the mid-1500s over one thousand print shops were operating in Europe. As printing improved over the next century, "true crime" books began recounting criminal acts and the brutal punishments that awaited those apprehended. The books satisfied a hunger for gore and provided warnings for potential offenders. It's probably worth mentioning that during this era public executions took place regularly in most European countries, attracting huge audiences for violent displays of state authority. By mid-century the modern novel was born with the publication of Samuel Richardson's *Pamela* (1741), which initiated the first public outcries over the effects of media.[13] Richardson's story of a virtuous servant girl preyed on by an unscrupulous seducer was excoriated in tracts circulated throughout London condemning it for lewdness and for assaulting "Principles of Virtue."[14]

The contemporary era of American media-violence debates begins in the 1960s. After decades of self-regulation, the media industries in the United States began reintroducing violence and sex that had been forbidden from film and TV by the production code in effect from 1930 to 1958. The production code had been written and enforced by the major movie studios to head off any regulation efforts by the government. With the decline of the Hollywood studio system following World War II, the structural underpinning of industry restraint loosened. Meanwhile, news coverage of the Vietnam War was bringing unprecedented levels of horrific imagery into living rooms across America. These combined factors made violent representation part of everyday life as never before. Movies either reveled in gore or used it to shock audiences in such crime thrillers as *Psycho* (1960) and *Bonnie and Clyde* (1967) or monster movies like *Night of the Living Dead* (1968). Director Sam Peckinpah even argued that he extended cowboy gunfight scenes in the western *The Wild Bunch* (1968) to force audiences to come to terms with the horror of combat. But nothing worried people like sex. Movies like *Who's Afraid of Virginia Woolf?* (1966) and *Blow-Up* (1966) used explicit language and graphic footage to push the boundaries of acceptable viewing to a breaking point. Recognizing that industry regulation could be just around the corner, the Motion Picture Association of America responded proactively by itself implementing a rating system that would evolve into today's G, PG, PG-13, R, and NC-17 system.

Debates over media sex reemerged in the "culture wars" of the 1980s. Conservative politicians and religious leaders worried about the nation's intellectual and moral standards turned their attention to entertainment and the arts, not to mention America's public schools. In the interest of restoring "traditional" values and standards, Reagan administration attorney general Edwin Meese led a now famous campaign to clean up popular culture from 1985 to 1986. Focusing primarily on sex, the infamous Attorney General's Commission on Pornography brought a great deal of attention to its own efforts but did little to change the entertainment industry and had no legislative impact at all. Some changes did occur in the music industry, largely triggered by two novel cultural forms of the era: MTV and hip-hop. Famously brought to life in music videos, evocative song lyrics provided the incentive for the formation in 1985 of the Parents Music Resource Center (PMRC) led by Tipper Gore and Susan Baker. Drawing on statistics showing rising rates of teen suicide and sexual assault, the group drew up a list of artists it termed the "Filthy Fifteen" for presentation to Congress. Asserting that performers like Prince and Madonna were causing documented harm to the nation's young people, the PMRC gathered sufficient support to enable the recording industry to move quickly to develop its own Parental Advisory labels before Congress could act. In a similar move, the TV industry launched a comparable voluntary labeling system in advance of the 1990 Television Violence Act.[15]

Soon medical and mental health professionals would weigh in. By the late 1990s, these groups had reached a consensus that media play a role in violence occurring at home and in the streets. A small yet influential list of widely publicized studies helped make the case, most notably the American Academy of Child and Adolescent Psychiatry's report titled "Children and TV Violence,"[16] which asserted that over one thousand studies "point overwhelmingly to a causal connection" between media violence and aggressive behavior in children.[17] As a meta-analysis, this joint statement had nothing to do with research conducted by either professional group; it simply relied on statements made elsewhere, which later would be proven statistically suspect. In a similar document emerging at this time, the American Psychological Association (APA) asserted that "there is no doubt that higher levels of viewing violence are correlated with increased acceptance of aggressive attitudes and increased aggressive behavior."[18] To its credit, the APA did not claim that media cause aggression, only that some kind of correlation could be identified. This meant that while troubled individuals might consume violent media, the material they watched could not be blamed for their behavior. Hence, the US Office of the Surgeon General elected not to list exposure to media as a cause of aggressive behavior among young people, adding further that it is "extremely difficult to distinguish between the relatively small long-term effects of exposure to media violence and those of other influences."[19]

Later worries about sex and violence on TV led to a law requiring V-chips in televisions made after 2000. This means that almost all televisions in use today contain V-chip technology. The problem is that the V-chips are hardly ever used because parents can't figure out how to negotiate the complex menus and controls required to activate them. Shortly after the introduction of the chip, a Kaiser Family Foundation study revealed that less than 15 percent of parents reported using it. The story is similar with Internet use. While just about everyone has heard about the purported dangers of Internet porn and the presence of pedophiles online, most parents either don't have monitoring software or don't know how to use the technology they have.[20] In the years since 2000, especially since 9/11, the media-violence debate has lost the frenzy of concern seen in the 1990s. A growing number of researchers have recanted dire predictions about the negative effects of violent movies and computer games, as scholars from the humanities and social sciences have added more nuance and complexity to the discussion.[21]

We Like to Watch

People take pleasure in media violence because it seems to take place in another world. It can be made aesthetically dazzling or even beautiful. Contemporary violent films use an elaborate array of devices that viewers have come to accept as real. Multicamera cinematography records action from many angles and perspectives; quick-paced montage editing heightens perceptions of fast movement and excitement; slow-motion segments draw attention into the scene and heighten the illusion of verisimilitude; Foley audio effects and dramatic music stir excitement further. All of this contributes to what Stephen Prince terms a "stylistic rendition of violence." Writing of Sam Peckinpah's stylistic renderings, Prince describes a three-part process of montage construction: "The relatively simple, slow-motion insert crosscut into the body of a normal-tempo sequence; the synthetic superimposition of multiple lines of action with radical time-space distortions in a montage set-piece; and montages approaching Eisenstein's notion of intellectual editing, wherein the viewer is moved to cognitively grasp psychological or social truths."[22]

Because people enjoy imaginary worlds filled with violence, works using violence become commodities. Whether one blames supply or demand, the market for media violence remains intact, vibrant, and growing. People like media violence, often for the wrong reasons. It gets attention quickly and spices up movies, TV shows, and games. It lives in the culture of masculinity, strength, and national might. Images of suffering can turn into objects separated from the thing itself. People look at the images without seeing the actual pain. This can have a number of effects. Roland Barthes believed that shocking images of human suffering send us the message that horror has already happened and is over. The pictures offer evidence of something the viewer will not experience. "Such images do not compel us to action, but to acceptance. The action has already been taken, and we are not implicated," Barthes writes.[23] Put another way, the images tell us that we are safe and that the violence in the picture has been done to someone else—often in a faraway land.

Artists and technicians make media violence attractive. And most viewers fully realize that a good portion of what they see isn't real. The photographer Alfredo Jarr has observed that the camera never actually documents the complete experience of what one sees.[24] It creates an abstraction of the scene it records. Perhaps it is this distancing effect that allows representations of violence to become great art. Horrific images can convey a transcendental meaning and even a certain beauty. In circumstances in which such images are in short supply, they can fetch top dollar from those willing to pay. But an overabundance of violent images can lessen their effect, contributing to a desensitization among viewers. When this happens, the particularity of a single story of tragedy can get lost in an ocean of represented suffering. We see this in news reports of natural disasters in which accounts of individual injury or death become multiplied into statistical reports of losses or, in the language of war reporting, into casual references to "collateral damage."

We know that accounts of violence have always animated the human storytelling impulse. Engagement comes from the anticipation and vicarious experience of danger. It's a bit like salty food: we know it's not good for us, but we like it anyway. Hollywood may profit from our appetite for violence, but we can't blame it for creating the hunger. Violence has always been with us as an ingredient in our most widely read fairy tales, our most highly attended movies, a lot of what we watch on television, and the video games kids most clamor to play. It's also worth noting that a good deal of what we perceive as violence on the screen isn't as gruesome as we might imagine. Sometimes what we are really experiencing is a spectacle of light and sound effects that gives us pleasure because cinematic violence has become so familiar to us. Audiences really crave the comfort of a familiar story. Network executive Leslie Moonves has noted that audiences really don't like ambiguous outcomes very much. "They do not respond to nervous breakdowns and unhappy episodes that lead nowhere," Moonves has said, adding that "they like their characters to be part of the action. They like strength, not weakness."[25] In other words, viewers prefer drama in stories—and violent imagery provides that drama.

Some directors have sought to upset audience tastes for violence with exaggerated techniques or unusual formats. Avant-garde cultural theorists had long speculated that audiences could be awakened from complacency with radically "new" ways of seeing the world. Could a movie shock an audience to such an extent? Sam Peckinpah said that his movie *The Wild Bunch* (1969) was meant as a form of metaphoric protest against the Vietnam War. In *The Wild Bunch* a band of outlaws robs a bank in Texas and later escapes to Mexico, only to face a confrontation with the Mexican military. One famous scene features a lot of gun fighting in which large numbers of people get killed. The violence is inescapably gory, so much so that many viewers complained that the bloodshed had seemed too "real." Film historians have commented extensively about this particular Peckinpah movie and the many innovations he used in its realization. *The Wild Bunch* stands as a canonical example of how cinematic artifice can convey the illusion of violence in viewers' minds. But more to the point, Peckinpah seems sincerely to have wanted to make people feel sympathy for the victims of war. He would state, "We watch our wars and see men die, really die, every day on television, but it doesn't seem real. We don't believe those are real people dying on the screen. The media has anesthetized us."[26]

Peckinpah borrowed some of his techniques from the work of Akira Kurosawa. In Kurosawa's filming, numerous cameras would catch the action from different viewpoints, and the footage was later edited into extremely short segments. Further heightening the dramatic effect, Kurosawa would insert slow-motion clips to pull viewers back into the scene. Also, Kurosawa used telephoto shots to draw attention to specific details in scenes. With a large budget from Warner Bros., Peckinpah successfully adapted these techniques to shoot a movie on a larger scale than Kurosawa could ever contemplate. Audiences were thrilled by *The Wild Bunch,* and the movie's influence on the craft of filmmaking is still evident today.

Crime and Punishment

Worlds of crime and war greet us every day in different forms. Entertainment and news broadcasts provide endlessly repeated accounts of threats or assaults. Some would argue that such material helps convince citizens of the need for enhanced police protection and tougher laws. While today the role of the United States as the unrivalled leader in entertainment production is being challenged, America remains well ahead of other nations in the commission of state-sanctioned aggression.[27] As it now stands, the United States is the sole Western nation to use capital punishment, with 74 percent of its citizens supporting the policy.[28] Even as crime rates have fallen during the past decade, prison construction has continued to accelerate.[29] Of the 2 million people in jail in America, nearly 50 percent are African American, and nearly three-quarters can't read.[30] Can we say it is a coincidence that most of the violent criminals we see in movies and TV are people of color?

Certainly media haven't created this situation. But can we speculate that stories of violent crime create an atmosphere of suggestibility? In his classic book *Public Opinion,* Walter Lippmann wrote that citizens can't themselves gather all the information they need to fully participate in a democratic society. Instead they look to different forms of media. These days three-quarters of Americans say that they base their opinions about crime on television and online news coverage.[31] Unfortunately, the mainstream media don't do a very good job of informing people about crime in a comprehensive way. Most of the nation would be quite startled to learn that crime is down in nearly every category for which records are kept. Since the turn of the millennium violent crime rates have dropped by 13 percent; yet television coverage of crime stories continues to show a steady increase.[32] As the occurrence of homicides has declined by 33 percent, coverage of homicides has risen by a stunning 473 percent.[33]

The reasons for these disparities between real and imaginary worlds are economic in part. As television networks have become absorbed subsidiaries of huge media conglomerates, shareholder demands for profits have grown. News entities compete with each other and with other kinds of programming for viewers. As a result they become splashier and more geared toward the spectacular. The consequences of this sensationalization are hardly neutral. They create the sort of atmosphere that enabled the nation's now familiar "three-strikes" laws, first initiated after the widely publicized kidnapping and killing of twelve-year-old Polly Klaas and the crusade-like media campaign that followed. In the 2000s the powerful effect of stories about victimized children led to the implementation of a system of statewide media alerts reminiscent of air-raid warnings. This occurred despite a decline in child abductions.

These misrepresentations of threats to the public create a culture of fear. Such an atmosphere creates tempting opportunities for politicians to use voter anxiety in their bids for office. How many times have we heard a candidate offering to hire more police or build a stronger military? Such promises can be very effective when people are frightened or feel at risk. These kinds of scare tactics have been in the news quite a bit in the first decade of the 2000s, especially in the United States. The aftereffects of 9/11 provided an opening for fearmongering of all kinds, and the arrival of terrorism on American soil provided additional opportunities for politicians in states along the Mexican border to blame rising rates of unemployment, welfare dependency, and educational failure on illegal immigrants entering the United States from the south. In recent years, states like Alabama, Arizona, and Georgia have passed draconian immigration bills, causing farmworkers to flee to other states in massive numbers.[34] This has led to tighter border controls and more stringent legislation in border states to punish undocumented workers—even though those very states depend heavily on such low-wage workers to keep their economies going.

Foreign policy and national defense also suffer from this propagation of misinformation. As topics disconnected from the lived experience of most citizens, international and federal matters are much more contingent on media representation. As the major networks have lost viewers, budgets for such programming as the ABC, CBS, and NBC evening news have dwindled. Original reporting through investigative journalism has lessened as reliance on reports issued by the government has increased. In some cases, the Pentagon now literally writes the news. Although much was made of Washington's media manipulation during Operation Desert Storm, television had for some time capitulated to government news offices, coming to rely on them nearly completely for certain kinds of content. Regardless of what one thinks about the war on terrorism, there can be no doubt that knowledge of federal antiterrorism efforts is limited to what Washington wants the public to know.

US forces finally located Osama bin Laden a decade after 9/11, brutally killing him on the spot. For years comedians and politicians had mocked America's failure to find the terrorist. Even critically minded filmmakers like Morgan Spurlock couldn't resist the joke (consider Spurlock's 2008 *Where in the World Is Osama Bin Laden?*). Navy SEALs executed the unarmed bin Laden without interrogation or trial—marking a significant departure from previous official US policy. Yet, despite protests by Amnesty International and Hamas, the American public joined much of the world in celebrating the event, as US military leaders proclaimed they would continue to hunt down and murder other terrorists in a similar fashion. The effects of 9/11 still haunt America and the world, as bombings continue to occur. We must remember that these horrific episodes have deeper roots in past events. But network news rarely provides much depth or historical perspective. With each new tragedy, connections are rarely made to the prior three decades of terrorist assaults on US holdings, the thinking behind the bombings, or US aggression in places like Afghanistan, Angola, China, Indonesia, Lebanon, Pakistan, Russia, Sudan, Syria, Turkey, and Vietnam. Violence begets violence, whether the victim is a small child or an entire nation. Breaking cycles of violence is difficult and may sometimes seem impossible. But we must always keep in mind that violence is not a natural behavior or an inevitable consequence of human conflict.

Notes

1. George Gerbner, "Reclaiming Our Cultural Mythology," *The Ecology of Justice* 38 (Spring 1994): 40.

2. Barry Glassner, *The Culture of Fear: Why Americans Are Afraid of the Wrong Things* (New York: Basic Books, 2010). See also Dan Gardner, *The Science of Fear: How the Culture of Fear Manipulates Your Brain* (New York: Plume, 2009); Jeff Wise, *Extreme Fear: The Science of Your Mind in Danger* (New York: St Martin's, 2011).

3. David L. Altheide, *Creating Fear: News and the Construction of Crisis* (New York: Walter de Gruyter, 2002).

4. Wole Soyinkka, *The Climate of Fear: The Quest for Dignity in a Dehumanized World* (New York: Random House, 2004).

5. Corey Robin, *Fear: The History of a Political Idea* (Cambridge: Oxford University Press, 2004).

6. Zygmunt Bauman, *In Search of Politics* (Stanford, CA: Stanford University Press, 1999), 5.

7. Seymour Feshbach and Robert B. Singer, *Television and Aggression* (New York: Jossey-Bass, 1971), 12.

8. Senate Committee on the Judiciary, *Children, Violence, and the Media: A Report for Parents and Policy Makers* (Washington, DC: Senate Committee on the Judiciary, 1999).

9. Realvision, "Facts and Figures about Our TV Habit," TV Turnoff Network, www.chamisamesa.net/tvoff.html (accessed May 2, 2011).

10. University of California, Santa Barbara, Center for Communication and Social Policy, "Executive Summary," National Television Violence Study (1998), www.ccsp.ucsb.edu/execsum.pdf (accessed May 21, 2011).

11. Karl Lorenz, *On Aggression* (New York: Harcourt Brace and World, 1963).

12. George Gerbner et al., "Growing Up with Television: The Cultivation Perspective," in *Media Effects: Advances in Theory and Research,* ed. J. Bryant and Dolf Zillman, 2nd ed. (Hillsdale, NJ: Lawrence Earlbaum, 2002).

13. See Harold Schechter, *Savage Pastimes: A Cultural History of Violent Entertainment* (New York: St. Martin's Press, 2005), 122.

14. In the next century photography would emerge to further exacerbate public anxieties about media and public morality. Violence was the centerpiece of early movies. Thomas Edison demonstrated the new technology in 1895 with his Kinetoscope film *The Execution of Mary, Queen of Scots,* a thirty-second clip of a beheading. Movies of boxing matches proved to be a sensation. The immediate success of *The Corbett-Fitzsimmons Fight* (1896) gave it the dubious distinction of being one of the first films to evoke the ire of anti-media-violence critics, a sentiment that led to a ban on prize-fighting movies in 1912. As in today's effects-laden action films, graphic depictions in movies like Sigmund Lubin's *Chinese Massacring Christians* (1900) or Georges Méliès *The Last Days of Anne Boleyn* (1905) were used to help show off the features of the moving image.

15. University of California, Santa Barbara, "Executive Summary."

16. "Children and TV Violence," American Academy of Child and Adolescent Psychiatry (AACAP), March 2011, http://aacap.org/page.ww?name=Children+and+TV+Violence&section=Facts+for+Families (accessed January 20, 2012). For earlier, more extreme warnings about media violence, see American Academy of Pediatrics and AACAP, "Media Violence Harms Children," in *American Academy of Pediatrics and the American Academy of Child and Adolescent Psychiatry's Joint Statement on the Impact*

of Entertainment Violence on Children—Congressional Public Health Summit, July 26, 2000 (New York: Lippincott, Williams, and Wilkins, 2000).

17. American Academy of Pediatrics and AACAP, *Joint Statement.*

18. American Psychological Association, as cited in James D. Torr, ed., *Is Media Violence a Problem?* (San Diego, CA: Greenhaven, 2000), 6.

19. Ibid., 7.

20. "FAQs and Statistics," National Center for Missing and Exploited Children, www.missingkids.com (accessed October 10, 2011).

21. In 2001, a group of media scholars asked the American Academy of Pediatrics and the American Academy of Child and Adolescent Psychiatry to reconsider their joint policy statement issued that year on media violence because of its "many misstatements about social-science research on media effects." The group of scholars, which included such notable intellectuals as Jib Fowles, Henry Giroux, Vivian Sobchack, and Pulitzer Prize laureate Richard Rhodes, cited the statement's factual inaccuracies and its "overall distortions and failure to acknowledge many serious questions about the interpretation of media violence studies." Subsequently a research subculture began developing around the examination of positive aspects of media and game culture. A notable example of this scholarship is represented in James Gee's *What Video Games Have to Teach Us about Literacy and Learning* (New York: Palgrave, 2003). In this work Gee takes a cautious look at the neurological processing skills that game technologies help develop, without leaping to the conclusions of more hyperbolic writers in this area like Steven Johnson, author of *Everything Bad Is Good for You: How Today's Popular Culture Is Actually Making Us Smarter* (New York: Riverhead, 2005).

22. Stephen Prince, *Screening Violence* (New Brunswick, NJ: Rutgers, 2000), 187.

23. As cited in David Levi Strauss, *Between the Eyes: Essays on Photography and Politics* (New York: Aperture, 2003), 81.

24. As cited in ibid., 91.

25. Lynn Hirschberg, "Giving Them What They Want," *New York Times Magazine,* September 4, 2005, 32.

26. Sam Peckinpah, quoted in Stephen Prince, "The Aesthetic of Slow-Motion Violence in the Films of Sam Peckinpah," in *Screening Violence* (New Brunswick, NJ: Rutgers, 2000), 176.

27. Hugo Adam Bedau and Paul G. Cassell, *Debating the Death Penalty: Should America Have Capital Punishment?* (Cambridge: Oxford University Press, 2004).

28. Ibid.

29. Ibid.

30. Ibid.

31. Lori Dorfman and Vincent Schiraldi, "Off Balance: Youth, Race, and Crime in the News," Building Blocks for Youth, http://buildingblocksforyouth.org (accessed July 10, 2011).

32. Ibid.

33.   Jennifer L. Truman, "Criminal Victimization, 2010," Bureau of Justice Statistics Bulletin, Bureau of Justice Statistics, www.bjs.gov/content/pub/pdf/cv10.pdf (accessed March 10, 2012).

34.   Scott Kersgaard, "Immigrants Already Beginning to Flee Alabama," *Colorado Independent,* July 18, 2011, http://coloradoindependent.com/94278/immigrants-already-beginning-to-flee-alabama (accessed July 18, 2011).

Chapter Eight
Globalization

Everyone has heard of "globalization" as a way of looking at the world as a big system. In recent years two important changes have taken place in how we view globalization, which suggest novel ways to address this book's discussion of worlding. The first change has to do with "real-world" geopolitical power and economics as we enter what has been termed the "post-American" age. The second change lies in the "imaginary" world of communications technologies like the Internet and mobile phone networks. Both of these shifts will have great influence over the kinds of worlds we inhabit. These changes are dynamic in that they are unfolding now and will continue to develop in coming decades. So, it's important to look to the future, to examine real and virtual world systems as they now exist and the directions in which they are moving.

Real-world globalization and conceptions of world systems date to the age of discovery, when nations were seeking to find new lands and to acquire resources. Colonial empires would emerge around the world, as powerful nations expanded into new territories. But the real beginning of globalization had to wait for the great world wars of the twentieth century. It took modern communications and industry to enable global consciousness and global conflict.

Following World War II the United States and Soviet Union emerged as the world's two great superpowers. Then the Soviet Union fell apart economically and politically, eventually breaking up into smaller, less powerful nations, leaving the United States as the world's remaining superpower. But the United

States soon began to falter in this role, largely due to the expense of fighting multiple wars in distant nations while buying more goods than it was exporting. In recent years, its own internal economic mismanagement nearly brought the US economy to the point of collapse. Meanwhile, other countries that did less fighting and had sizable populations continued to build their economies. In particular, the so-called BRIC nations of Brazil, Russia, India, and China have grown to become genuine players in the world economy, and some observers believe they will dominate by 2050. While the United States remains the world's largest consumer and by far the most powerful military power, we have entered a "post-American" era in which American values, products, and interests need to share the stage with those of other countries, which may eventually become consumer and military leaders as well.

Imaginary-world globalization is technological, emerging from the growth of the Internet and related communications like satellite TV, GPS devices, and mobile phones. Many of these changes are obvious; others are subtler. The simple fact that Internet technology allows us to inhabit new worlds has become a widely experienced part of everyday life, although it's worth noting that the World Wide Web is ubiquitous only in nations with evolved telecommunications. Underdeveloped nations in many parts of the world still lack basic phone service for large segments of their populations and so do not fully share in the global communications age. But the broader effects of new network technologies are truly revolutionary. It's funny when we look to the past and consider all the speculations made about our current age. Futurists predicted air travel, computers, enhanced weaponry, and space exploration—but no one really could imagine the phenomenon of personal computing linked with communications technology. IBM chairman Thomas Watson famously declared in 1943, "I think there is a world market for maybe five computers."[1]

Society was in many ways unprepared for the emergence in the last two decades of the virtual universe. And it's a phenomenon that continues to unfold right before our eyes. Just when we had become accustomed to e-mail, Web surfing, and online gaming, everything went mobile, once again warping our relationship with real and imaginary worlds. A decade ago, one left one's body at one's desk when traveling in cyberspace. Now virtual experience travels with us in continual interaction with the real world. GPS-enabled smartphones can us help find the way home or locate toothpaste in the local Walmart. Games can link our real-world bodies with virtual environments. A kind of convergence is taking place that calls for new paradigms in the millennial age.

Resources and Crises

This book has been a journey through many kinds of worlds, both virtual and real. I began this project many years ago because I had become fascinated with the human impulse to travel in the mind—and it seemed to me that the ways one could do this were getting increasingly vivid and more and more intense and immersive with each passing year. All of this made me wonder whether our expanding capacity to travel to imaginary realms was a good thing in an age of global crisis. After all, one doesn't need to look very far to find some expert or concerned group arguing that television, games, and whatever the latest diversion might be damage us, or hold the potential to damage us, especially the youngest and most vulnerable in our society.

But then I realized that in a very profound sense, all of our understandings of the world are, in fact, products of mental processes. As we can learn from great philosophers and children at play, the world we experience is only as vivid or real as our capabilities for apprehending it. Our minds allow us to see only what we know how to see, or as Plato would put it, only the reflection of some "reality" that we can never fully perceive. Should this worry or depress us? Not necessarily. But with this realization come challenges and opportunities.

The most pressing challenge lies in the fact that we all see the world differently. Not only do we each have our own imaginary worlds, but we all have acquired different stories, lessons, and experiences from our vastly varied genetic dispositions, cultural backgrounds, family histories, economic situations, educations, and job experiences. We may all share some common aspects of what Northrop Frye called the "educated imagination," but then we often disagree as well.[2] It's fair to say that most people want the same basic things in life—family, friendship, comfort, safety, and security—although our definitions of these things might vary wildly. But as I've discussed in this book, there exist certain truths, certain common things that we can say about each other, even in a world where we have learned to know and value our many differences. We all want a good life. We all seek a better world. And if we can find a way to locate that impulse in each other, we will have accomplished a great deal. After all, this is what all the great religions and political philosophies have sought to accomplish: to bring us together somehow, to demonstrate that despite our innate sense of ourselves as individuals, despite the alienation that we may at times feel about the world around us, we are at the end of the day social creatures.

And we must be this. Why? We must understand our interconnectedness because we have but one place to live, one planet. In ancient times the idea of a global community didn't matter much. Society was local, and the world people knew extended only as far as they could travel. But as the world has advanced, especially in recent decades, the globe has become smaller and more connected. We know about our neighbors in ways we never did a generation ago. And our technologies, our means of communication, our economies, and our weaponry place new responsibilities on us. More importantly, the world has become increasingly aware of its own limits. It is one planet after all, with only so much oil, water, food, and clean air. So we arrive at a discussion as this consideration of worlding draws to a close: What do we do about our world, our real world?

How many times has one heard the familiar saying "Think globally and act locally"? The expression is attributed to United Nations environmental advisor René Dubos, who used the phrase in 1972 to advocate the principle that social change should start at home. Not only is it daunting for individuals to consider changing the world, Dubos said, but we also need to remember that change takes place in "unique physical, climatic, and cultural contexts."[3] The think globally, act locally idea is often used to convey the notion that individual actions are most recognized in the small groups and communities where they take place. It's a way of overcoming the discouragement that many people feel in the face of huge institutions that seem to govern their lives.

Let's face it: there are many times when many of us feel that the world's problems are just too big for any of us to solve. How much can one vote count in a national election? What does it matter if I recycle a few aluminum cans or turn off the water? It takes millions of people to do anything important. Only big institutions affect the world in any meaningful way. Of course, our civic-minded selves may then remind us that it is large masses of people acting in concert that pressure corporations and governments to act. But the thought is daunting nevertheless. It's no accident that people think this way. From early childhood, we are taught that forces beyond our immediate control govern the world. One must learn the rules and adopt one's behavior to systems beyond one's control and understanding. Violate the rules, and there will be trouble. Acting out is a symptom of immaturity.

Where do these attitudes come from? In part they emerge from a social realization of how regions composed of millions of people need to be organized to avert chaos. It's necessary for everyone to have the same response to a traffic light to avoid traffic accidents on a massive scale. But perceptions of a big world and the smallness of individuals can have other, less productive effects as well. In an age of modern communications media, the one-directional flow of information doesn't allow people to talk back in any meaningful way. Big corporations make the goods we buy. Governments determine the laws that control our lives. Giant political parties select our leaders.

In yielding to forces beyond their control, people learn to recognize and validate institutions of power. In many ways this is a useful and positive way of relating to the larger society around us. But the workings of organized of power and control can make people feel helpless and impotent in managing their own lives. In the face of overwhelming authority, political constituents can come to believe that institutional structures are immovable, change is impossible, and participation in the political process is a waste of time.

Mass media play an important role in reminding people of the scale of institutional power. Complimenting images of huge systems of control are messages that focus attention on individual interests, which narrowly define how human worth is defined. Great importance is placed on being oneself in a world of conformity. Constant attention in the media to celebrities, wealthy people, and other "winners" suggests that good looks, public recognition, and the accumulation of possessions are the standards by which success in life is judged. This focus on surface appearance and material acquisition undermines any collective awareness. Stressing values of solitary achievement and competition, we are told to put ourselves before others. Personal ethics, social responsibility, and connectedness are easily overwhelmed by an ethos of self-involvement and solitary interest.

It's difficult to admit that most of us glean large portions of our understanding of the world from what we see on TV or read on the Internet. Most people don't get to travel to different lands or even around much of the United States. We learn about distant places and other people from what we acquire from the media. Aside from debates over the objectivity of these impressions, there are more fundamental questions about what it means to be an observer rather than an active participant in the mediascape. The observer role implies a certain passivity and an inability to control what is being observed. We see the world as others see it for us. We cannot question how it is seen or even what is seen. Inevitably, this produces a sensation of distance from the world represented in images. It is no accident that people often describe real-life events as seeming just like a movie. Media images have become so ubiquitous in our lived experience that they become the standard against which we measure reality. News events like wars and elections take on an otherworldly quality. People trust that they really are taking place but think that such occurrences are far removed from their personal lives. What difference does it make to my life if a soldier dies in a distant land or people are starving? Does it really matter who gets elected? Why bother to participate?

The good news is that increasingly people are choosing to participate. Across the United States and around the world, citizens of nations of every kind are taking up the challenges that face them. Despite the alienating elements of contemporary life—a mind-numbing media, huge institutions, and life defined by consumerism—people still act, still believe, still participate. Some might argue that this willingness to take action is inherent in human nature, perhaps a survival mechanism. Others might say that the world is finally recognizing the enormity of the threats it faces, as the depletion of our environment and global resources becomes more and more apparent. Or it may simply be this: deep within each of us lies a recognition that life matters, other people need us, and the conditions to support a healthy existence require some attention. In these final pages of *Worlding*, I examine briefly a few of the challenges facing our global ecology and discuss why we have reasons to be optimistic about our future.

Peak Oil

In recent years, as gasoline prices skyrocketed, people were finally shaken into a realization that economic news can affect them. The world now faces the genuine possibility that it is reaching "peak oil"—the point at which global oil resources begin to decline permanently. The British Petroleum (BP) oil spill in the Gulf of Mexico, resulting from an accident on the *Deepwater Horizon* drilling platform, showed how desperate energy companies have become in their search for alternatives to oil imported from the Middle East. Within a year of the BP incident, a variety of factors pushed gasoline prices to new record highs. This was the first time for many that a national issue—America's dependence on "foreign" oil—actually touched their lives. It was particularly meaningful that it concerned fuel, because natural resource issues rarely get much public attention. With the rise in gas prices, the problem was not so much a shortage of oil as a manipulation of the price by the nations that supply the United States. But the price hikes focused attention, if only momentarily, on the world's reliance on fossil fuels.

The gasoline price panic and media frenzy it created tell us much about the way environmentalism is framed and distorted in public discourse. As the price of gas topped $4 per gallon, television news suddenly was filled with images of price signs and interviews with frustrated customers. Angry commuters and truck drivers complained about the bite a tank of fuel took out of their wallets, as newscasters spoke of the detrimental effect of high prices on vacation driving. The news value of the issue became reduced to the kind of stories that broadcast journalists could illustrate with easily found images that spoke to how most people experienced the problem in their daily lives. Less discussed and visualized were the underlying causes of price hikes, which derived from international oil markets, the economic issues involved, and the attendant political pressures. Explaining the complexities of such matters was simply too time-consuming and unphotogenic for a two-minute segment on the nightly news. At best, some reports featured fleeting images of ghutrah-clad sheiks at a meeting table who had inexplicably "decided" to impose the punitive price on the Western world. Middle Eastern nations like Iran, Iraq, Kuwait, and Saudi Arabia inevitably were portrayed as greedy and generally irrational suppliers of the fuel vital to Western industry and agriculture. The story of international oil thus was abstracted and decontextualized from its history and politics.

Oil became a major international issue in the years leading up to World War I (1914–1918), when Britain, France, and Germany each held colonial interests in what is now the Middle East. The advent of the twentieth century marked the transition of military forces in Europe from horse-drawn to mechanized vehicles. Army trucks, tanks, and airplanes suddenly needed oil-derived fuel. Vast fields of petroleum had recently been discovered in Persia (present-day Iran) and Mesopotamia (Iraq). To this day Iran, Iraq, Kuwait, and Saudi Arabia supply the vast majority of the world's oil. To secure this valuable resource during World War I, British forces swept across Iraq in 1916, outmaneuvering the French and gaining control of Mesopotamia. The United States soon worked with Britain and France to push Germany and its Ottoman Empire allies out of the region. In a sense, the history of Middle Eastern discord is the history of modern Western society's demand for fuel.

The opening of Middle Eastern oil fields to American interests occurred a few years after the 1911 breakup of Standard Oil, which had secured an effective monopoly on petroleum in the United States. Owned by the Rockefeller family, Standard Oil eventually was divided by the US Supreme Court into thirty-four new companies, thus establishing the corporate structure of today's oil and gasoline industry. The new companies included, among others, Continental Oil, which became Conoco; Standard of Indiana, which became Amoco; Standard of California, which became Chevron; Standard of New Jersey, which became Esso (then Exxon); and Standard of New York, which became Mobil. Rockefeller owned stock in all of them.

The United States is by far the world's largest oil consumer, gobbling up more than double the amount used by the second-largest user, Russia. Oil consumption by China is growing more quickly than for any other nation, however. Since 2000, China's oil needs have more than doubled. For the best part of the past century, most oil went for transportation uses. As the US automobile industry boomed in the post–World War II years, gasoline was consumed without restraint. But in the 1970s, political turbulence in the Middle East threatened to disrupt the region's oil sales to Western nations. Relations had always been prickly between Israel (established in former Arab territory following World War II) and its neighboring countries of Egypt, Jordan, Syria, and their allies in the region. Almost immediately after Israel's establishment in 1948, Arab nations began to discriminate against their remaining Jewish populations. In 1956, Egypt blocked ships going to Israel, setting off the first Arab-Israeli war. Israel retaliated with military action, resulting in a pattern of mutual aggression that would persist for decades. Early in this process, oil-producing countries recognized the influence they could assert by collectively withholding oil from larger and more militarized nations. In 1960, Iran, Iraq, Saudi Arabia, and Venezuela formed the Organization of Petroleum Exporting Countries (OPEC), which was later joined by eight other nations. An Arab-Israeli war took place in 1973, resulting in a shutoff of Arab oil exports to Israel and its allies, like the United States and Britain. This created the famous US oil crisis of the 1970s, when drivers had to wait in long lines to get service from gas stations. In 1977, the United States completed a pipeline from Alaska to help ease its reliance on Middle Eastern oil.

The oil crisis of the 1970s had one important benefit to the United States. It made the nation's drivers finally take seriously the concerns of environmentalists, who had been arguing that inefficient car engines were burning too much gas and polluting the country's skies. States with lots of cars, like California, began passing laws to force automobile manufacturers to design smaller, more fuel-efficient vehicles. Foreign car companies responded more quickly than the heavily bureaucratic and union-bound US auto industry. Soon American roads were filled with compact Volkswagens, Toyotas, and Datsuns, as emissions controls were built into the engines of all kinds of automobiles. The energy savings of small cars and emissions-control technology couldn't solve the problem of more and more cars on the road, however. Eventually automakers needed to address the issue of petroleum fuel altogether. This has prompted development of vehicles powered by electricity—a concept fraught with challenges. Demand for electric cars has been insufficient to bring their price down to that of gas-powered models. In part, this is due to the short range of current batteries and inconvenience of recharging them, which takes much longer than filling a gas tank. Hence, gas-electric hybrids have been the option of choice. But their engines are more complicated and problem ridden than those of conventional cars, causing some manufacturers to offer free maintenance as a sales incentive.

Making cars more fuel efficient can't fully compensate for the increasing energy needs of a growing world. Between 1950 and 2012, the world's population has more than doubled, from 2.5 billion to 6.8 billion people. While much has been done to help ameliorate the consumption of oil and gas in transportation, home, and industrial use, tremendous amounts of petroleum are used in agriculture, mostly in the production of fertilizer. Decreases in oil supplies can cause higher food prices and produce famines in poor or highly populated countries. By some current estimates, the world's population is already too large. According to geologist Dale Allen Pfeiffer, to return to a sustainable level and avert disaster the US population would have to be reduced by at least one-third and the world population by two-thirds.[4]

Oil spills have produced another kind of petroleum-related environmental problem. Until the mid-1990s, tanker ships ruptured on a regular basis, often releasing millions of gallons of oil into oceans. The scale of some spills was such that cleaning them up required months and even years. In addition to polluting waters and coastlines, the ocean-born petroleum killed birds and marine mammals on a massive scale. Such accidents prompted worldwide building standards for oil tankers involving double hulls. These measures largely eliminated the occurrence of oil spills from ships.

As the world looks to the future of oil consumption, one central issue remains unresolved: no one knows for certain how much oil remains to be extracted from the Earth. Various interests in the oil debate offer quite contradictory estimates of how much oil exists and how long the world can continue consuming it. OPEC asserts that global oil reserves equal 1.3 trillion barrels, an amount that will exhaust itself in thirty to forty years at current consumption rates if no new deposits are discovered. The 1.3-trillion-barrel figure derives from the reserves stated by OPEC nations and others, which use a variety of formulas to estimate the amounts. Not all nations are able to prove their estimates by any scientifically verifiable means, and others have been raising and lowering their estimates with the passage of time. In some cases estimates have proved to be overstated. In other places new supplies of oil have been found. Considering all these variables, the long-term outlook for petroleum is muddled, placing even more importance on the development of alternative energy sources and improved conservation techniques.

Water and Starvation

Most people in industrialized nations never think about water. Yet shortages of water for drinking and irrigation constitute one of the world's greatest sources of suffering. Water is another essential natural resource whose supply causes worldwide concern. Although oceans cover two-thirds of the Earth's surface, methods for removing salt from seawater remain expensive and thus impractical for satisfying the world's freshwater needs. Agriculture accounts for 70 percent of world water use, with industrial and household consumption each taking 15 percent. In geographical terms, water is most available in North America, Europe, and northern Asia, leaving South and Central America, Africa, southern Asia, and Australia with water challenges. About half the world's population lives with a piped source of water to homes, with 40 percent existing without modern sanitation systems and 20 percent with no natural water supply at all. Frustrating the problems caused by the uneven natural water distribution is the poverty of many nations in Africa, South America, and southern Asia. Many poor nations lack both sufficient drinking water and water to grow crops. Lack of water is the major cause of food shortages. Aggravating the situation further is the nonessential expenditure around the world of large volumes of water for swimming pools, car washes, landscaping, and golf courses.

Making matters still worse are the many forms of water pollution. For decades homes and industries released sewage and manufacturing waste into water sources without restraint, fouling many of the world's rivers and lakes. Contaminants from agricultural insecticides, herbicides, and fertilizers created further problems. Until environmental regulations put a stop to such practices, the waters of the American Great Lakes were famous for being undrinkable and hazardous to swimmers. In addition to such pollution by human beings are natural factors that ruin water. Some of Africa's most water-starved countries have water supplies ridden with bacteria and insects. The dracunculus, more commonly known as the guinea worm, is prevalent in over a dozen African nations like Ghana, Nigeria, and Sudan. People drinking unfiltered water unknowingly consume the microscopic parasites, which flourish in ponds and wells. Inside the human digestive tract, the worms grow to up to three feet in length, then migrate to the skin, where they emerge through blisters. Through the efforts of philanthropic groups like the Carter Center and The Bill and Melinda Gates Foundation, the guinea worm has been eradicated in many countries. But in other nations, it remains but one of several waterborne threats to public health.

Shortages of water most directly affect food supplies. According to the United Nations, twenty-five thousand people die of starvation every day.[5] Approximately 800 million are undernourished, a number that has grown with the outbreak of blight that has decimated wheat fields in Africa and Asia. At the other end of the spectrum, over 1 billion people worldwide are considered overweight. In poor nations with chronic food shortages, populations often suffer conditions like diarrhea, edema, and skin rashes, as well as catabolysis, which occurs as the body breaks down muscle and fat tissues to keep vital systems going. Starvation victims in warm climates frequently grow too weak to recognize thirst and become dehydrated. Psychologically, starvation victims also can become apathetic and withdrawn, losing the will to help themselves. Ironically, most experts say that the world produces sufficient food to feed its entire population. The problem is distribution. Some nations can't afford to buy the food they need, while others are blocked from importing it by political turmoil or war. Efforts by the United Nations and some countries have helped ameliorate food shortages somewhat. The United Nations estimates that the percentage of undernourished people in developing nations has declined from 20 percent in the 1990s to 12 percent in 2012. UN officials assert that with continued effort, the number of underfed people in the world can be reduced from 20 to 10 percent by 2015.

World Climate Change

Can human activity alter the climate and temperature of the Earth? Few topics have received more public attention and generated more controversy than global warming. The term refers to the rising average temperature of the world's water and air near sea level. Most experts agree that this temperature has increased approximately 1.3 degrees Fahrenheit during the past one hundred years, a phenomenon attributed to air pollution primarily caused by the burning of fossil fuels. Global warming theorists believe that as high-altitude layers of gas grow denser, they interfere with the dissipation of heat rising from the Earth's surface. The effect is like that in a greenhouse. Scientists believe that this buildup of "greenhouse gases" has been taking place since the beginning of the Industrial Revolution in the 1700s, but only in recent decades has it begun to affect the Earth's climate. To stop the buildup of greenhouse gases, experts have advocated tougher air-pollution standards in industry and transportation. Whether to implement these often expensive changes has been the topic of much political debate. Proponents of global warming stand on one side, predicting polar ice melts, rising sea levels, floods, droughts, and damage to living organisms from heat and exposure to solar radiation. Opponents argue that such concerns are unproven and overstated.

Given the strength of scientific evidence for the threats posed by global warming, national governments and many corporations around the world have taken the matter seriously. In 1997 the United Nations organized a historic meeting on global warming in Japan. Called the Kyoto Protocol, the resulting agreement called for nations to collect data on climate change and to adhere to certain air-pollution standards. In the years since the Kyoto meeting, 190 nations have signed the accord. But because some of the signatories have not ratified the agreement, only 60 percent of polluting countries are in compliance. The United States, which creates the largest share of the world's pollution, is among the nonratifying nations.

Why would anyone object to such a treaty? The United States, Canada, and Australia argued the Kyoto Protocol was too strict and unfair because it didn't insist on full compliance for a number of poor countries.[6] Some European nations thought that the agreement didn't go far enough and was thus ineffective in actually protecting the world's environment. In its most recent Human Development Report on climate change, the UN estimated that unless the world's output of greenhouse gases is cut in half by 2030, countries will be obliged to spend as much as 20 percent of their budgets to offset the effects of climate change.[7] To achieve such a reduction the United Nations has said that the world's most wealthy nations need to reduce their emissions by 80 percent. But few governments seem to be heeding these warnings.

Aggravating the situation are vocal opponents who deny the threat of global warming altogether. Corporations that would need to spend money on pollution controls sometimes take this latter position. Commentator Rush Limbaugh is famous for characterizing environmentalists as overprotective whackos who seek to inflict extremist views on innocent businesspeople. As Limbaugh wrote in his book *See, I Told You So,* "Despite the hysterics of a few pseudo-scientists, there is no reason to believe in global warming."[8] Though Limbaugh offers no objective evidence for such flamboyant assertions, his audiences often revel in his audacity, as well as in a spate of recent books with titles like Grant R. Jeffery's *The Global Warming Deception: How a Secret Elite Plans to Bankrupt America and Steal Your Freedom.*[9]

These anti-environmentalist sentiments have an ironic effect on public opinion. On a theoretical level, environmentalism is concerned with the interconnectedness of human endeavors. It looks at the products and actions of human beings and asks questions about their effects and uses. Yet, in popular discourse, environmentalists are often seen as radical activists or "special interests" concerned with preserving exotic species or putting limits on activities that give us pleasure. Part of the problem concerns the enormity of the environmentalist cause. It's difficult on an individual level for any of us to see the effects we may have on pollution or resource depletion. And it's easy for anti-environmentalists to assert that one person's actions don't make a difference. After all, many people already believe that their actions are insignificant in relation to those of the millions of other people in the world.

In response, groups like Greenpeace stage attention-getting interventions to focus public attention on environmental issues. The history of Greenpeace is significant in charting the evolution of the contemporary international environmentalist movement. The group originated in the early 1970s in reaction to US nuclear weapons testing in Alaska. Activist Bill Darnell thought of the name that combined "green" with "peace" to convey the group's concerns over environmental destruction and armed conflict. In 1978, Greenpeace launched its original ship, *Rainbow Warrior,* to disrupt the dumping of waste in oceans and to interfere with seal and whale hunting. Over three decades, Greenpeace has staged numerous protests and blockades on land and sea, taking action, for example, against the Kimberley-Clark Corporation for its destruction of ancient forests to manufacture Kleenex and Cottonelle products. In many instances, Greenpeace has succeeded in generating attention for an issue on its own terms. But just as often, actions by Greenpeace and similar groups are seen as expressions of overheated minority opinion.

Science and Belief

In an age in which large segments of society distrust leaders and experts, it is no surprise that on certain issues people prefer commonsense answers over intangible theories. In the case of global warming, this mistrust takes the form of a bias against scientific explanations for changes in the world's climate. Much anti-environmentalism stems from a growing tendency of popular opinion to dispute anything that can't be verified by "real-world" experience. But many global warming skeptics also are choosing between two "imaginary" world views—one scientific and one religious—for things that can't be confirmed readily by real-world observation. Disputes between science and religion have deep roots dating to the Enlightenment (1500–1900), when people first began in large numbers to question magical explanations for phenomena like gravity, planetary movement, and the shape of the Earth.

For many people, "belief" in God as the controller of natural phenomena was—and remains—preferable to scientific views on issues like evolution, conception, and gender roles. But such thinking generally has been confined to fundamentalist populations and exerted little influence on public policy. With the election of George W. Bush to the presidency in 2000, however, things changed. Bush launched a variety of "faith-based" initiatives and began a campaign to reform government in more religious terms. Among other things, he eliminated many environmental regulations and expressed disbelief in global warming. He also revoked government-funded medical research that used embryonic stem cells on the grounds that unborn fetuses were fully formed people in God's eyes. Bush sought to stop all abortions on these grounds. On taking office in 2009, President Barack Obama acted quickly to reverse these decisions.

Schools remain major battlegrounds in the contest between religious and secular interests. Rather than attempting to remove science from education, Christian creationists sought to introduce religious accounts of natural phenomena to "balance" curricular offerings. In philosophical terms, the efforts seek a return to the pre-Enlightenment science of the kind that existed before the separation of science, theology, and philosophy that took place in the Western world in the 1700s. Competing against the modern naturalistic, mechanistic view of the world would be an older way of thinking that featured belief in supernatural power, magic, and theology. The focal point of creationist educational reform lies in the teaching of "intelligent design," which asserts that the world and its civilizations emerged from God rather than physics or natural selection.

The term "intelligent design" first received attention with the US Supreme Court's 1987 *Edwards v. Aguillard* ruling, which found that the mandatory teaching of creationism in Louisiana violated the US Constitution. Creationists responded that because scientists had disagreements about the origins of the universe, religious accounts should be included in education to fully represent the "controversy" over evolution. Creationists adopted the "intelligent design" term because it sounded nonreligious. The US National Academy of Sciences responded in 1999 that "intelligent design, and other claims of supernatural intervention in the origin of life" could not be weighed equally with scientific views because they could not be tested by experiment or proven by empirical means.[10] This hardly put the issue to rest, as recent political contests have shown.

Disagreements over the teaching of scientific ideas in schools do not stop with evolution and creationism. Virtually all aspects of school curricula dealing with reproduction and sexuality have provoked controversy for many years. Teen pregnancy and sexually transmitted diseases continue to threaten American youth, especially those who do not understand the basic facts of conception and disease transmission. Most feminists and progressive educators argue that the best way of addressing these problems lies with fully explaining the body and its workings to young people. Conservatives and religious groups counter that such teaching implicitly sanctions early sexual behavior. To conservative groups abstinence is the only acceptable doctrine. Because state and local authorities largely govern school curricula, these disagreements have resulted in a wide disparity in the knowledge base of young people about conception and sexually transmitted diseases.

On a global scale, issues of reproduction and contraception define population growth. Currently the world population stands at approximately 6.8 billion—an increase of 500 million in the past decade. Continued growth in the world's population is attributed in part to medical advances and increases in agricultural productivity since the 1960s. The United Nations Population Division predicts global population will reach 9 billion by 2050. Nine countries are projected to account for half the increase: Bangladesh, China, Ethiopia, India, Nigeria, Pakistan, Republic of Congo, Uganda, and the United States. Efforts at population control have been growing with the wide-scale use of contraception. China's one-child policy is an example of government-mandated population control, although the practice has brought allegations of forced abortions and infanticide. In most cultures decreases in birthrates have been linked to higher levels of education among women. The US government currently budgets approximately $300 million per year for reproductive control, 90 percent of which supports family-planning clinics. In the United States and throughout the world, some religious faiths oppose family planning using contraception.

Overpopulation remains a matter of great global concern, although debates about the issue go back several hundred years. In his 1798 *An Essay on the*

Principle of Population, Thomas Malthus argued that populations grow until food resources can no longer support them.[11] Malthus noted that this limitation on population had occurred in past civilizations and predicted it would happen again in the 1850s. These dire forecasts were not realized—at least not on a global scale. But uneven distribution of food resources has claimed millions of lives, especially in African nations. Ultimately, issues like overpopulation, world hunger, and resource management become concerns for all the world's governments. Such problems suggest that nations can no longer continue to think only of themselves. This is difficult in a world defined by the boundaries and priorities of nation-states, which often exist in conflict with one another. This need for global thinking prompted the founding of the United Nations following World War II. The various UN agencies represent a vital mechanism for considering the world as a whole by looking beyond the interests of individual states.

The Post-American World

American patriotism and national pride have always touted the United States' unique place in world history—from its founding days as a novel "experiment" in democracy to its current role as the world's strongest military power. Given the challenges facing the globe, the question facing the United States is whether it will be part of the solutions or the problems. Is the United States a member of the world community or does it stand defiantly alone? Obviously there is no question that America has a great impact on the rest of the globe: its combat strength remains unrivaled; the nation's economic influence is profound; America's culture sets trends everywhere; many argue that US-style freedom stands as a model for other countries to emulate. At the same time, many argue that the United States puts it own security before others', exploits trading partners, wastefully consumes, shamelessly pollutes, and manipulates weaker nations. With these conflicting identities, America's cultural division hits the international stage.

Partly America is governed by the belief that it is different from other nations and unique in its place in history. These ideas date to Revolutionary times, when Alexis de Tocqueville wrote in *Democracy in America* of the special configuration of the United States as a nation of immigrants and a laboratory for egalitarian governance.[12] De Tocqueville wrote, "The position of the Americans is therefore quite exceptional, and it may be believed that no democratic people will ever be placed in a similar one."[13] Proponents of American exceptionalism argue that the

United States is extraordinary in that it was founded based on a set of democratic ideals rather than a common heritage, ethnicity, or ruling elite. President Abraham Lincoln said in his Gettysburg Address that America is a nation "conceived in liberty, and dedicated to the proposition that all men are created equal."[14] In this view, America is inextricably identified with opportunity and freedom.

In theory, America governs itself through a system of checks and balances, designed to prevent any person, faction, region, or government entity from becoming too powerful. States maintain a partial independence from federal rule. Congress and the White House must agree on major legislation. Proponents of American exceptionalism argue that the distrust of concentrated power prevents the United States from suffering a "tyranny of the majority" and also that it allows citizens to live in localities whose laws reflect their residents' values. The consequences of this political system are seen in laws that can vary greatly across the country, as well as in the often frustrating transfer of political power from one party to another in the electoral process. Critics argue that the party system sometimes limits the ability of diverse groups to influence American politics.

Even the most generous interpretations of American exceptionalism have been distorted in recent decades by assertions that the United States holds itself above other nations and sees itself as an "exception" to international law. Hence, the United States has launched unprovoked military attacks against sovereign states, excluded itself from global environmental agreements like the Kyoto Protocol, held prisoners in contravention of the rules of the Geneva Convention, and frequently ignored admonitions from the United Nations. These behaviors have raised doubts about the character of the United States as a world citizen. But regardless of whether one agrees or disagrees with how the United States conducts it foreign policy, one thing is certain. The world is changing in dramatic ways. America must adapt to these changes.

What is the appropriate role for the United States in the world? In *The Post-American World,* Fareed Zakaria writes of three "tectonic shifts" taking place in the world during the past five hundred years. The first was the rise of the Western world, a process that ran from the fifteenth through the end of the eighteenth centuries. In other words, this shift occurred with Enlightenment-era advances in science, industry, agriculture, commerce, and communication. The second shift took place in the closing years of the nineteenth century, with the rise of the United States and its expanding economic, military, and political leadership. The third great shift Zakaria calls "the rise of the rest." Over the past few decades, countries all over the world have been experiencing once unthinkable rates of economic growth. This brings him to one inescapable conclusion: at the politico-military level, we remain a single-superpower world, but in every other dimension—industrial, financial, educational, social, cultural—the distribution of power is shifting, moving away from American dominance. That does not mean we are entering an anti-American world. We are moving into a post-American world, one defined and directed from many places and by many people.[15]

Hope and the Future

The world faces numerous challenges. Many forces push people and nations apart: their differing histories and cultures, opposing belief systems, competition for resources, and political conflicts. At the same time, *Worlding* has tried to point out ideas that bring us together: common wants and needs, the imperative to share limited resources, the benefits of communication, and desires for fairness and equality. Perhaps the most important antidote to alienation is the human potential for self-analysis and the opportunity that history occasionally provides for new ways of thinking. In our individual lives, our collective experiences, and our national journey through time, there remains the perpetual promise of a fresh start. As we move through the second decade of the twenty-first century, the world faces the opportunity of a new day.

And there is cause for optimism. *Worlding* has addressed the wide variety of imaginary and real worlds we carry in our minds and experience in daily life. At the same time, this book has tried to point out certain consistencies in human thinking—having to do with things we all need and value. In his recent book *Blessed Unrest,* Paul Hawken writes of a unifying spirit among human beings.[16] He speaks of the many challenges and wrongs the world has seen through the ages. In doing so, he notes a consistent pattern in human societies facing challenges and correcting wrongs. Just over two centuries ago, three-quarters of the world's population was enslaved in one way or another. But we changed that with the birth of social justice movements—and later civil rights movements, peace and justice movements, and all manner of movements to make the world a better place.

This is the living presence of the utopian imagination. In these movements we find a living manifestation of that primal yearning for "something else" that makes people today question authority, business, and government. Currently more than 2 million organizations exist worldwide to address one issue or another. To Hawken, all of this activity to fix the world is part of a burgeoning groundswell. But rarely does one hear about this growing movement, this tidal wave of humanity looking for a "something else." Partly this is because the utopian imagination that unites people around the world in a common struggle follows no standard ideology, no single issue or political party. One single people, or one nation, or even one group of countries does not own this utopian vision. In Hawken's words, "The movement grows and spreads in every city and country, involves virtually every tribe, culture, language, and religion, from Mongolians to Uzbeks to Tamils."[17] It comprises families in India, students in Australia, farmers in France, the landless in Brazil, banana workers in Honduras, the "poor" of Durban, villagers in Irian Jaya, indigenous tribes in Bolivia, and housewives in Japan. Its leaders are farmers, zoologists, shoemakers, and poets. It provides support and meaning to billions of people in the world. "The movement can't be divided because it is so atomized—a collection of small pieces, loosely joined. It forms, dissipates, and then regathers quickly, without central leadership. Rather than seeking dominance, this unnamed movement strives to disperse concentrations of power."[18]

Conventional news media don't report on this movement because it is too large and diverse to represent in a compressed format. More often, voices of unrest are labeled as insignificant or interested only in special interests. As a result the voices of agitators, environmentalists, academics, the poor, the aged, the young, indigenous people, liberals, and others are discredited. This takes place in part due to deep philosophical structures that still guide most of humanity. The Enlightenment may have provided much in advancing science and our faith in the capacities of the human mind, but it also left a residue of binary thinking, of believing that reality could be divided into categories like mind and body, good and evil. This gave rise to big ideologies, training us to believe that single doctrines could guide or save us.

But the end of the end of the twentieth century saw the collapse of big ideologies. In the great clashes and wars among fascists, Communists, and proponents of liberal democracy, everyone lost. The twentieth century resulted in more bloodshed and misery than any time in history, with over 100 million people losing their lives in over 160 wars. And those decades also saw the greatest rate of environmental destruction in all of recorded time. Thus the utopian imagination I am describing is not simply a literary idea or a philosophical dream. The great rising up of humanity against authoritarianism has roots in suffering and destruction on a global scale.

It is impossible to overcome division without acknowledging the interdependence of people and nations. Interdependence implies mutual responsibility and a commitment with others to a common set of principles. This concept differs distinctly from "dependence," in which some are reliant on the actions of others, and "independence" in which historical actors act alone. As Martin Luther King Jr. wrote, "Injustice anywhere is a threat to justice everywhere. We are caught in an inescapable network of mutuality, tied in a single garment of destiny. Whatever affects one directly, affects all indirectly."[19] An interdependent framework implies that all participants are materially and ethically reliant on each other. This is the prescription for overcoming the division and inequities that divide people against each other.

And so a movement grows from a deep tradition of compassion for fellow human beings and a vision of the world as a living organism. Two centuries ago, Immanuel Kant and Jacques Turgot saw humanity as such a system. They were not alone in viewing the world as a living organism. From Spinoza to Gandhi, from Lewis Thomas to Teilhard de Chardin, philosophers, religious teachers, and scientists have all wondered if the entire human race might be integrated in mysterious and inexplicable ways. "Joined together, the great mass of human minds around the earth seems to behave like a coherent, living system," wrote Thomas.[20] Put somewhat differently, we may well be seeing what Gary Snyder called the "great underground," a unifying set of beliefs and hopes that can be traced throughout human history to healers, priestesses, philosophers, monks, rabbis, poets, and artists "who speak for the planet, for other species, for independence, a life that courses under and through empires."[21]

One World

If a primordial consciousness guides us in the quest to sustain life on the planet, there is ample evidence that our newest technologies may also be of help. As Jane McGonigal points out, the impetus toward social networking and computer gaming that is sweeping the planet may well bring virtual and actual worlds together in very positive ways. In recent years, the online industry has recognized that the appeals of Internet connectivity—communication, sharing, collaborative networking, and task-oriented play—can be harnessed for productive social ends. Indeed, tens of thousands of websites, mobile phone apps, and new games have been popping up all around the globe to tackle real-world problems like world hunger, poverty, energy shortages, and social alienation. The most important positive function of the Internet is to bring us together as human beings, not push us apart. With a new generation of computer games that are feeding millions around the world and helping scientists find cures for humanity's worst diseases, we can no longer say that technology is stealing a generation of young people from the "real" world. "We are hardwired to care about reality," McGonigal writes, "with every cell in our bodies and every neuron in our brains."[22]

So where does this leave us? We stand here today amid the glorious potentials of worlding, a concept as old as human consciousness yet enlivened in the present moment in remarkable ways. Everywhere we find ways to imagine and build new worlds, traveling to the outer reaches of fantasy and adventure, linking networks of friends and social contacts, experiencing unknown realities in virtual environments. But as the human yearning for otherworldliness pulls us, we also recognize the sobering reality of the world we actually inhabit. In this real world, life does not advance with a mouse click or the push of a button. A person needs to act, to do things, to make a life for him- or herself—and even to change the world.

Notes

1. "Thomas J. Watson," Wikipedia, www.en.wikipedia.org (accessed January 3, 2012).

2. Northrop Frye, *The Educated Imagination* (Bloomington: Indiana University Press, 1966).

3. René Dubos, quoted in Joy Grillion, "Think Globally, Act Locally," CAPITA, http://capita.wustl.edu (accessed February 4, 2009).

4. Dale Allen Pfeiffer, "Eating Fossil Fuels," From the Wilderness, 2004, www.fromthewilderness.com/free/ww3/100303_eating_oil.html (accessed September 25, 2012).

5. "Food and Agriculture Organization of the United Nations," Wikipedia, http://en.wikipedia.org/wiki/FAO (accessed June 11, 2011).

6. "Canada to Withdraw from Kyoto Protocol," BBC News, December 13, 2011, www.bbc.co.uk/news/world-us-canada-16151310 (accessed January 5, 2012).

7. "Fighting Climate Change: Human Solidarity in a Divided World," Human Development Report 2007/2008, United Nations Development Programme, http://hdr.undp.org/en/media/HDR_20072008_EN_Overview.pdf (accessed February 10, 2011).

8. Rush Limbaugh, *See, I Told You So* (New York: Pocket Books, 1993), 171.

9. Grant R. Jeffery, *The Global Warming Deception: How a Secret Elite Plans to Bankrupt America and Steal Your Freedom* (New York: WaterBrook, 2011).

10. *Science and Curriculum: A View from the National Academy of Science,* 2nd ed. (Washington, DC: National Academy of Science, 1999).

11. Thomas Malthus, *An Essay on the Principle of Population* (New York: Penguin Classics, [1798] 1999).

12. Alexis de Tocqueville, *On Democracy in America* (New York: Harper Classics, [1835, 1840] 2006).

13. Ibid.

14. "Full Text of the Gettysburg Address," *Internet Archive,* http://archive.org/ stream/gettysburgaddres00linc/gettysburgaddres00linc_djvu.txt (accessed October 21, 2012).

15. Fareed Zakaria, *The Post-American World* (New York: W. W. Norton, 2008).

16. Paul Hawken, *Blessed Unrest: How the Largest Movement in the World Came into Being and Why No One Saw It Coming* (New York: Viking, 2007).

17. Ibid., 11.

18. Ibid., 12.

19. "Letter from a Birmingham Jail," Wikipedia, http://en.wikipedia.org/wiki/ Letter_from_Birmingham_Jail (accessed February 11, 2011).

20. Lewis Thomas, as cited in Hawken, *Blessed Unrest,* 142.

21. Gary Snyder, as cited in Hawken, *Blessed Unrest,* 5.

22. Jane McGonigal, *Reality Is Broken: Why Games Make Us Better and How They Can Change the World* (New York: Penguin, 2011), 266.

INDEX

ABOUT THE AUTHOR

David Trend is Professor and Chair of the Department of Art at the University of California–Irvine. Formerly the editor of *Afterimage* and *Socialist Review*, he is the author of numerous books, including *Everyday Culture: Finding and Making Meaning in a Changing World* (Paradigm 2008), *A Culture Divided: America's Struggle for Unity* (Paradigm 2009), and *The End of Reading: From Gutenberg to Grand Theft Auto* (Peter Lang 2010).